Internal Coaching
Stories of Success in Organizations

Edited by
Dr. Anne Power

Moon-Gazing Hare
PUBLISHING

Electronic & print book design by Unauthorized Media
Cover design by 2Faced Design

ISBN: 978-0-9960512-4-8

Contents

Acknowledgments

Many colleagues and friends, too many to list here, encouraged this undertaking, and I thank them for their support. Yet others were willing to invest time and effort in a completely speculative project. This group coalesced in response to an email I sent to a number of my former Columbia Coaching Certification Program students and fellow faculty members, soliciting input.

Sue Negrey and Margaret Walsh joined in from the start. They have been my coeditors, organizers, friends, and, most of all, believers. Without these two committed CCCP alums this book would not have been launched, and so Sue and Margaret deserve particular thanks.

Writing (and re-writing) is hard work, and each contributor to this book has earned special gratitude from me:

- Pat Armstrong, for tirelessly and enthusiastically going the course. Pat and her coauthors Stephanie Duignan, Denise Verolini, Nancy Amick, and Lorilee Mills produced such a thoughtful, analytical, and absorbing narrative of the Wells Fargo wealth management's group internal coaching practice that we realized we had not one, but three full chapters of content we did not want to abridge.

- Alan Polansky, who has pushed the cause of coaching forward in his organization since his graduation from the first CCCP cohort. Alan's chapter describing his efforts in Eastern Europe reads like a novel. More important than his contribution to this book, however, is his impact on the employees of AmRest, for his commitment to changing from command-and-control leadership to a coaching mindset. Alan is one of the most dedicated coaching advocates I've had the honor not merely of working with, but of calling a friend.

- Marsha Borling, for being a thinking partner long before this book ever happened. Marsha helped envisage the concepts of Coach Principled Leadership. Going forward, Marsha has led teams in hospital systems, embracing the challenge of the changes in health care, and ensuring that her teams' executive leadership was visible and available.

- Lou Chrostowski, whose continued commitment from the beginning helped turn the CCCP into a true learning community. Lou's belief in the power of coaching in organizations has been strong throughout a long career of external and internal coaching.

- John Schuster, for contributing to the field of coaching before it was a field. For being willing to join the CCCP faculty team before the CCCP curriculum methodology was developed. For giving new coaches the courage to go below the surface with their clients. And, most of all, for being a friend from the onset of our careers.

- Katheryn Wankel, for diligently covering the expanse of assessments "out there" and updating her chapter as she waited patiently for the 2nd Edition. Katheryn is one of the most dedicated CCCP alumni volunteers, generously assisting with whatever is needed to further advance the Program.

- Rachel Ciporen, whose scholar practitioner mindset is valued by our learning community, is evident in the classroom, and is clearly expressed here in her chapter on 360 Degree Feedback. As one of Rachel's colleagues, I am fortunate to be the recipient of the wisdom she brings to our team. Our friendship is a treasured gift.

- Stefan Hendricks, for reaching out to his business colleagues in order to explore the possibilities for coaching change leaders. Stefan has covered the globe as a consultant and now as a coach he shares his business acumen and expertise in his chapter.

I also would like to thank my friend and colleague Terry Maltbia, the director of the CCCP program. We worked together creating the content, criteria, and curriculum for the program—then, as now, based at Columbia Teachers College—but it was Terry whose insight led him to reach out to the Columbia Business School for joint ownership of the program. This dual identity has been key to the success of CCCP. Terry's passion and commitment to situating coaching in a theoretical base, developing curriculum so that it stood on firm ground, is the reason our program is considered one of the best in the world. Thus, nearly half our

CCCP participants cross an ocean—or the Equator—twice a year to learn how to coach. They then take the CCCP coaching philosophy and methodology back to their home organizations in Europe, Asia, Africa, or South America.

Thanks, too, go to the employers and clients of our chapter authors, for being willing to share best practices. Because of the camaraderie of the CCCP alumni and their belief in the transformational power of coaching, our contributors came together here to tell the stories of change driven by coaching: within divisions, across entire organizations, in individual careers, and in lives. Their employer organizations, appreciative of the benefits derived from coaching, have been extremely generous in granting permission to share these successes.

I thank Anita Buck for being an extremely devoted, hysterically fun and enormously skilled editor, committed to working with me and all the authors in a patient, kind, and straightforward way, who became a friend in our tandem effort to pedal this project across the finish line. I am also pleased to thank book designer Chris Derrick, who came to the project just as we finished polishing the copy, and made our book beautiful in multiple formats.

There are many people who worked with the project early on—Gerald Cauley, Suzanne Jacobson, Jane Taylor, to name a few—whose input has proved invaluable. I also am grateful to the various individuals and teams I have worked with during my career, on whom I learned to coach before it was called coaching. I think of many of you more often than you know.

Finally, I must thank my family and friends outside coaching for supporting me in this effort by not bugging me with "How's the book going?" They all know my "one out of every five ideas comes to fruition" philosophy, and when I start something new they give me the freedom without judgment to try new ideas. Some ideas fail, some don't. This one didn't.

Introduction

Coaching is the hottest trend in leadership today. And yet, only ten years ago, "executive coaching" was widely viewed as a last resort before a manager was asked to leave the organization. The reality, though, was that many executives who were essentially forced to accept coaching greatly enhanced their work performance and salvaged their careers. At the same time, many executives hired coaches directly to address a variety of personal agendas and coaching goals. Following this trend, a number of early adopter organizations began providing coaching to select upper level executives as coaching came to be seen as executive development—a perk rather than a rebuke.

A cadre of coaching advocates, some of them CEOs with personal experience of coaching, believed that an organization could integrate coaching in a more strategic way and to better advantage. Common coaching practice to this point had been to hire a coach, what we now call an "external coach," from outside the organization. At that time the role of the external coach was to focus on the coaching client's agenda; as a result, the client's improved performance would benefit the organization. But what if, these coaching advocates reasoned, an organization established its own in-house coaching practice to widen the scope of coaching and to align individual clients' goals with the goals of the business?

It is this question that the organizations discussed in this book are still answering. "Internal coaching"—coaching that originates within the organization and enhances particular leadership behaviors identified by the organization—is so cutting-edge that it has, in fact, only begun to coalesce as a distinctive set of practices.

These practices are rarely discussed as deeply and incisively as among the graduates, participants, and faculty of the Columbia University Coaching Certification Program (CCCP), where I teach as a founding faculty member. Established in 2007, the first certification program emphasizing coaching within an organization, CCCP is regarded as the leading program of its kind. This book is an outgrowth of the CCCP professional practice community, now in its twelfth cohort with several hundred attendees to date.

I am often asked by current participants, as well as by program alumni, to facilitate connections for them across program cohorts and with faculty members. Over the last few years I've connected with external and internal coaches around the globe to share best practices, information, and stories about coaching in organizations. It thus became apparent to me that there was a need to collaborate as a community of practice to share knowledge and bring best practices to the larger coaching community, and that one way to do this would be to collaborate on a book.

So, some of us wrote a book. Or rather, different members of the CCCP coaching community wrote the chapters they would have liked to have read earlier in their careers. These chapters are in effect how-to's and go-to's, written by experienced coaches who lead coaching efforts within organizations. In most cases, the authors are the people who actually led the initiatives discussed in the first four chapters, the case studies. They describe applied skills and practices: how the methods and theories work on the ground, how practitioners adapt their knowledge base to each client, organization, and situation. The chapters are filled with success stories, essential steps, and obstacles to avoid.

Read together, the subject chapters provide a readily comprehensible overview of coaching across the organization. Because none of us coach in a vacuum, we have not aimed the chapters solely at coaching practitioners. We have taken care that the information will also be useful to anyone in an organization who has anything to do with employee development—for example, executives implementing or considering a coaching program, as well as human resources professionals.

Here are our topics:

The chapter "Wells Fargo: The Evolution of a Coaching Culture" is a case study of the Wells Fargo wealth management group's establishment of an internal coaching culture. It examines the organizational context, culture, and readiness for change prior to implementation, and discusses the foundations of the coaching culture, the importance of executive sponsorship, and the actions for cascading the coaching culture across the organization.

"'Wszystko jest możliwe' ('Everything is possible'): Coach Principled Leadership in Eastern Europe" concerns AmRest Holdings SE (AmRest, WSE: EAT), today the largest independent restaurant operator in Central and Eastern Europe, which was founded soon after the former member nations of the Communist Bloc opened to free trade.

"Team Coaching in Health Care" anticipates the increasing opportunities for this type of practice; as management teams proliferate, the performance of the members as a group, not just as individuals, often needs refinement. This chapter describes a successful and practical five-phase approach to team coaching, illustrated with client experience.

"The Internal Executive Coaching Process at Wells Fargo Wealth Management" continues the saga of this Wells Fargo unit's internal coaching program, discussing its implementation and best practices, including how coaches are chosen; funding, contracting and goal setting; and the actual work of coaching, including the challenges inherent in an internal program.

Even organizations with established internal coaching programs need to hire external coaches when appropriate. "External Coaches: Assessing an Organizational Client" is a how-to chapter discussing the factors an external coach should consider when designing, implementing, managing, and assessing external coaching engagements for organizations. Careful evaluation of these factors will help the external coach decide whether to accept the engagement, and, if it is accepted, will increase the level of success and value to the organization.

"Adventures in the C Suite: Coaching Executives" addresses the transformational nature of coaching. This chapter draws on the author's decades of experience coaching senior executives. While coaching is not psychotherapy, he encourages coaches to attend to the psychological dimensions of the process.

"Contracting for the Coaching Engagement" is devoted to the special considerations involved in establishing clear goals and boundaries for coaching engagements that take place within an organizational setting. This chapter defines contracting as an essential pre-coaching process, and recommends a series of questions designed to identify and integrate the goals and expectations of all the stakeholders.

"Using Assessments for Executive and Organizational Coaching" draws on the author's 25 years of experience growing leadership pipelines and transitioning leaders in, up, and around two major New York City financial institutions. She provided 360 Feedback and coaching for a major part of her career and in this chapter shares some lessons and best practices around those experiences.

"Multi-Rater Feedback in Executive Coaching Engagements" provides an overview of best practices and key considerations for Human Resource, Talent Management, and Organizational Development professionals as well as executives and external & internal coaches to consider when evaluating or developing their approach to 360-coaching.

"How Executive Coaching helps Businesses Transform" examines how executive coaching contributes to the success of business transformations. This chapter suggests several best practices about how coaches can help change leaders both personally and with the business transformation.

For me, this book is a chapter in a story that began twenty-five years ago. At that time I served on the board of the American Center for International Leadership, the premier organization for introducing emerging leaders of the world to their counterparts around the globe. Each board member served as a designated liaison for one of the countries; our role was to lead groups of up to three hundred leaders from the U.S. to that country. My country was the USSR, and on my first trip the summer of 1989 we went to Moscow, Sochi, and then all the way to Siberia to visit Novosibirsk. I was assigned an interpreter, Igor, by one governmental body and a spy by another—the KGB. The interpreter was a necessity, and the spy a "tag along" almost always within earshot.

After a few days in Moscow I began to notice that someone was going into my room. I imagined it was my spy, Viktor. One evening our entire group went out for dinner and then dancing in a large venue (there were almost no restaurants or clubs at the time) with the Muscovites. Typically, Igor would translate for me. However, on this evening, during an exchange with Viktor, Igor threw up his arms and said, "Talk for yourself!" before walking away. From that point forward Viktor spoke to me in fluent English whenever no one else was around; he had attended a school on the East Coast of the United States. Viktor admitted to going through my belongings and apologized, saying he didn't know what he was looking for, but that it was his job.

I next took a delegation to Russia in late 1991. No spies were assigned to us. The residents of Saint Petersburg had recently voted to reclaim its historic name from the Soviet-era Leningrad. Even more recently, after the failed coup of August 1991, the constituent republics of the USSR had declared independence and the Soviet Union was no more. When we arrived in Moscow we drove by toppled statues of Stalin—a sure sign this was going to be a different kind of trip. Standing in the middle of Red Square, I knew I was watching history unfold.

In 1991 there was no global economy as we know it today. A small group of us met with the leadership of Moscow to discuss boards of election (I was the director of a Cincinnati BOE) and locally elected school boards (I was also president of the Cincinnati Public Schools Board of Education). At one point early in the meeting, the mayor and treasurer got into a rather passionate conversation, which we Americans sat and watched. Evidently, these officials had met with representatives from the Coca-Cola company just prior to this meeting. After some minutes, the mayor turned to Igor (who was again my translator) and directed a question to me about Americans. He said, "Aside from the fact that there is no way to sell land for a factory"—there were no deeds, they could not yet sell land—"don't these Americans know we already have a Pepsi-Cola plant?" I said that in the United State there are many kinds of soda drinks. He retorted they didn't need Coke, they already had Pepsi. In this meeting, as in Red Square, I felt deeply aware of the enormity of the change that was occurring before my eyes.[1]

Fast-forward to 2010, when I flew to Poland to work with Alan Polansky, the author of the "Wszystko jest możliwe" chapter. Alan's intention was to fight the command-and-control leadership style that continued to permeate his organization. As an alumnus of the Columbia Coaching Certification Program Cohort I, Alan was on a mission to bring coaching to AmRest, and he had arranged a coaching skills workshop for the C-suite and next level of leaders. The training was held at AmRest headquarters in Wroclaw. Alan, John Schuster (fellow CCCP faculty member, book author, and author of the "Coaching Executives" chapter) and I led the program. More than thirty attendees, including the CEO and COO, spent four days learning and practicing the coaching competencies. On the last day of the session one of the junior leaders shared how meaningful the sessions were for him, saying as he held back tears that, as a boy growing up under the arm of Soviet communism, "It never occurred to me that someday I would be told to be a nice guy—to listen, ask questions, be curious." During this trip I realized again that I was watching history in Eastern Europe shift one more time.

The alumni of CCCP are changing workforces around the globe one person at a time, one team at a time, one leader at a time, one organization at a time. It is for that reason that the authors of this book had the enthusiasm, the perseverance, and the commitment to make it happen.

1. According to Anders Aslund, a senior fellow at the Peterson Institute for International Economics, "Coca Cola, McDonald's, Proctor and Gamble are very big and very happy in Russia." Nancy Marshall-Genzer, "U.S. Trade Feels Little Love from Russia," Marketplace radio feature, 2:03, aired August 7, 2013, http://www.marketplace.org/topics/world/us-trade-feels-little-love-russia.

1

Wells Fargo: The Evolution of a Coaching Culture

Patricia M. Armstrong, Nancy J. Amick, Stephanie Duignan,
Lorilee M. Mills, and Denise P. Verolini

Our organizational journey began with a business executive's request that went something like this:

> At a time when our business was growing rapidly, we placed big bets on some of our talented individual contributors by promoting them into leadership roles with the best of intentions but not much of a safety net. Most have had no formal leadership training and are clearly in need of additional support if they are to succeed in these stretch roles. As a young manager I benefited from some structured leadership training. What can we do to give these highly motivated, but untested leaders some management fundamentals and a greater chance of success as they work to help our business be more profitable?

Thus, as part of a comprehensive leadership development strategy, the Wells Fargo wealth management group began to develop an internal coaching culture. With much forethought, and moving in increments, the introduction of executive coaching was grounded in our organization's overall culture and fully aligned with achieving business results. Because of wealth management's focus on leadership development, in 2009 the five authors of this chapter entered Cohort III of the Columbia Coaching Certification Program. Each was coaching internally at the time and the goal of the CCCP training was for the coaching staff to have common grounding in a professional, university-based program.

Organizational Context

At the time it initiated its leadership development effort, Wells Fargo's wealth management group had 6,000 employees, a number that reflected a tripling in size over a three-year period in the mid-1990s. The business continued to grow, through a combination of mergers, acquisitions and organic growth, to more than 10,000 individuals by 2013. Wells Fargo (WF), a large U.S. financial services company, has also grown through mergers, acquisitions, and organic growth, and is now a workforce of more than 270,000 distributed across a wide range of specialty businesses in the financial services industry.

It is important first to understand the cultural context of the WF wealth management group and why, in this business, it is critical to give attention to its leaders. To a certain extent, the features of banking products such as checking accounts, credit cards, lines of credit, and even trust and investment accounts are somewhat commoditized. What generally differentiates financial services firms one from the other are the expertise and service orientation of its people rather the financial products themselves. This is particularly true in wealth management—a relationship-based business in which clients seek expertise to help guide future-oriented planning: lifestyle and retirement goals, wealth transfer to future generations, philanthropic endeavors, etc. The success of such a business is grounded in the ability to attract the best minds in specialties such as trust and estate planning, investment management, and custom credit who are able to engage with clients effectively and build long-term relationships with them and, by extension, with the firm.

Since the late 1990s a great deal has been written about the war for talent among wealth management firms, including the observation that leaders and managers play a vital role in both the recruitment and retention of professional talent. Much has also been written about the phenomenon of professionals leaving their managers in search of an organizational climate where leaders will be more attentive to their desire for personal and professional growth. It was in this competitive landscape that the first and then succeeding business head of the WF wealth management group delivered a call to action for more intentional development of the business's leaders and managers.

FOUNDATIONS OF THE COACHING CULTURE

Keeping in mind the goal of the business head, whom we'll call Mr. A, to provide results-based management training, we kicked off the leadership development initiative with the introduction of Situational Leadership[1] to the executive team, primarily because this was a model Mr. A had been exposed to early in his career and found practical and easy to understand. The executive team's training was followed by the introduction of the Situational Leadership model to the top one hundred leaders in the organization.

SITUATIONAL LEADERSHIP

In its simplest form, Situational Leadership presents the idea that employees learn and approach their work differently at various points in time, and that managers are more effective if they meet each employee where he or she is at that moment, i.e., the employee's approach to learning, level of experience in the current role, level of motivation, etc. The fundamental message behind this model is that leaders will be most effective if they adapt to the needs of the employee—not the other way around. As the business leaders came to understand and adopt this approach, the precursors of a coaching culture were beginning to take hold.

INTRODUCTION OF 360 FEEDBACK AND COACHING

Concurrent with being offered theoretical grounding in leadership development, the executive team was also given the opportunity to participate in an Advanced Leadership Seminar (ALS),[2] originally designed as a corporate-wide experience offered to Wells Fargo's high potential leaders, enabling them to learn more about themselves and how others perceive them. Through a week-long intensive program, roughly twenty peer leaders from across the company received what was often their first experience with 360 feedback from bosses, peers, and subordinates, delivered by an individual coach.

One of the key principles behind the design of this seminar is that strong leaders have the ability to candidly reflect on their own leadership behaviors, understand their impact on others, and adjust their behaviors to become more effective. For roughly a decade prior to the work described here, promising leaders from across the company were invited to this seminar as a signal of the organization's view of them as high potential, and to provide an in-depth learning experience focused on leadership. Wells Fargo senior executives often reference the significant role this experience played in their development as leaders.

The WF wealth management group's executive team participated in a dedicated version of ALS and then, just as we had done with Situational Leadership, we began cascading this experience to the next hundred leaders in the group. The ALS seminar not only provided a high-impact experience for these individuals, but created a cohort of leaders who began sharing information with each other and their respective teams about their leadership journey. It became desirable to participate in ALS and to follow up with those who provided feedback (the 360 raters) on the participants' commitments to try out new approaches and behaviors in response.

Talent Review and Succession Management

Wells Fargo has a longstanding practice of conducting annual talent and succession planning reviews. Each business unit begins this process with a comprehensive review of the depth and breadth of its leadership and professional bench in relation to its strategic business objectives. Leadership potential, strengths, and development needs are candidly discussed. The conversations progress to division-wide reviews, and conclude with presentations to the corporate CEO on the strength of each business unit's bench, as well as the talent within each unit who show potential to move between units and up within the corporation, i.e., people for the CEO and other business heads to get to know.

Within the wealth management group, the talent and succession reviews focused attention on the leadership bench—specifically, on the challenge of placing leaders who were successful as individual contributors or in small team lead roles into stretch assignments. Leaders thought to have high potential were continuing to receive training in situational leadership and offered the opportunity to attend an ALS seminar, but more was needed. A common assessment read something like, "Great at execution, drives for results, but has trouble commanding the room . . . . needs to work on engaging their team." Some authors on the topic of leadership have referred to this skill as the ability to create followership.[3]

Leading with Impact: Know Yourself, Know Others

After researching potential ways to address the need for leaders to more effectively create followership, the leadership development team concluded that a critical skill for leaders is understanding how others experience them and how those perceptions affect engagement—a highly personal skill that requires willingness to solicit and listen to direct feedback, then use that information to modify their approach. A two-day seminar called Leading with Impact[4] was designed to explore two questions:

1. What kind of impact do I have as a leader?

2. Is this the impact I need to have in order to lead and grow my business?

The foundational concept of the Leading with Impact (LWI) seminar is Know Yourself, Know Others—i.e., the idea that leaders need to understand themselves beyond their business skills and latest financial accomplishments. The seminar focused on the "how" of communicating a strong message (e.g., tone of voice, eye contact, body orientation) rather than the typical "what" or content of the message. The concepts of executive presence, ability to influence others, and capacity to sustain a high level of engagement were examined in depth. The seminar explored territory most leaders find somewhat unsettling, and covered training content somewhat atypical in a corporate setting.

The business case for addressing these interpersonal skills stated in part:

> Being smart, strategic and driven gets you in the door… the winning formula is about the unique ways in which you create an environment where your teams, business partners and clients keep coming back to you for more, in part because of who you are and the quality of the relationships you are able to develop and sustain.

Mr. A's successor as business head, Mr. B, was also a strong believer in this business case, and kicked off each small (twelve-person) seminar with introductory comments and examples from his own leadership journey, thus establishing the precedent that it would be both expected and acceptable to share personal vulnerabilities with the seminar facilitators and participants.

As in the Advanced Leadership Seminar—considered a prerequisite—the Leading with Impact seminar included a round of 360 feedback, using the same 360 feedback tool[5] so leaders could gauge how much they had been able to "move the dial" on the areas previously identified as strengths and opportunities. By design, the seminar comprised leaders from different geographies who typically were meeting each other for the first time. To deepen the 360 feedback, which synthesizes data gathered from people outside the seminar cohort, we incorporated peer feedback throughout the new seminar, including sharing candid first impressions of each other.

To strengthen the participants' ability to have positive impact with others, we introduced videotaping as the cornerstone of the LWI seminar. An organization[6] specializing in coaching for high-impact communications designed the videotaping sessions, coaching leaders to refrain from their usual business talk; the goal was simply to engage their audience of peers. Seminar participants identified two or three key behaviors on which to concentrate; they were to share these with their direct managers, who were to support these leaders' efforts to have greater impact with their teams.

ESTABLISHING AN INTERNAL EXECUTIVE COACHING PRACTICE

The timing of the Advanced Leadership and Leading with Impact seminars didn't always coincide with a new leader's first few months in a stretch role—a time critical to engaging the leader's new team.[7] Since ALS was a prerequisite to LWI, it could take up to a year to complete both, so the leadership development team needed a strategy to support early engagement between leader and team.

There was precedent within Wells Fargo for engaging an external executive coach for leaders in particularly critical roles, but Mr. B was also focused on the importance of creating a common organizational culture across the business and viewed an internal coaching process as one of the key ways to accomplish this. Mr. B believed that we are all works in progress—a belief he frequently communicated, and that was instrumental in creating a culture where coaching came to be viewed as an "I get to" rather than an "I have to."

Organizational Culture and Readiness

The early work with the wealth management executive team set the stage for viewing leadership development activities as a positive experience to be shared with others. Through Mr. B's explicit emphasis on development, learning, and growth, the next level of business leaders became more willing to talk about their mistakes, their lessons learned, their leadership journey, and the development work in which they were engaged.

This evolution stands in contrast to an organizational culture in which leaders are defensive, don't take responsibility for their actions, blame others, aren't willing to learn from mistakes, and are competitive in a way that causes those who are open and collaborative to feel threatened. Another key aspect of a culture less conducive to growth has to do with whether leadership development activities, including coaching, are perceived as a remedial rather than a developmental strategy, i.e., something that poor performers receive on their way out the door.

Wells Fargo clearly fostered a climate in which people and leaders were perceived as the company's most important assets and an investment to be developed, as an excerpt from the company's widely publicized "Vision and Values" illustrates:

> Our success depends on how much our team members care for their customers, for each other, their communities and our stockholders. People commit themselves to other people, not organizations. Processes are important but they don't do the work. People do. Because we believe in people as our competitive advantage, we'll continue to invest in our "human capital." It's the most important, valuable investment we can make ....[8]

Executive Sponsorship

In addition to the larger company's vision and values, Mr. B worked proactively to develop a culture that valued the recruitment and retention of strong talent. In Mr. B's view, people strategies are at the heart of the unit's ability to execute business strategies that have at their core a highly differentiated and team-based service model. It is within this organizational context that internal coaching was the next logical step in a comprehensive system of leadership development.

Mr. B was able to clearly articulate the purpose of developing an internal coaching capability and to link coaching to the goals and strategy of the business. As someone willing to share his own experience with coaching, Mr. B consistently sent the message that seeking coaching is not only acceptable, but fundamental to the growth and development of an effective business leader. He reinforced these views by investing in an expanded leadership development team that would include expertise in executive coaching.

ORGANIZATIONAL STRUCTURE

Establishing a formal internal coaching program requires planning and management. This function is typically located within a human resources, organizational development, or leadership development unit, or may be part of a corporate university. Some organizations engage a pool of internal coaches from disciplines across the organization and deploy them to specific coaching engagements as part of their primary business role. Experience suggests that a critical variable in the establishment of an internal coaching function is to ensure that internal coaches report outside the chain of command of those whom they coach so as to differentiate executive coaching from the normal coaching done by managers.

Because Mr. B viewed executive coaching capability as an integral component of his business strategy, the internal coaching function was located within an independent and dedicated leadership development team that reported to the wealth management group's human resources leader. The team is focused solely on leadership development activities and does not have any other human resources or business responsibilities. This dedicated team focus is critical to maintaining the clear boundaries and confidentiality needed to provide an effective internal coaching capability.

Also by design, the leadership development and coaching practice manager has direct access and accountability to Mr. B, who is actively involved in every aspect of the coaching function from recruitment— i.e., interviewing potential coaches for organizational and cultural fit, including business acumen—to prioritizing the queue for executive coaching based on business needs, such as hiring a new business leader from a competitor. Being able to quickly adapt to the wealth management group's evolving needs through direct connectivity with the business head and business strategy has been a critical variable in sustaining the relevance and viability of the internal coaching function.

CASCADING THE COACHING CULTURE

The group's success in introducing, then sustaining internal coaching at the senior leadership level led us to the next logical question: How can we cascade the benefits of coaching throughout our sales leadership organization? As the recipients of executive coaching, our senior leaders experienced firsthand how coaching could transform their leadership effectiveness and business performance and saw great value in developing their own coaching capabilities. In fact, word was getting out about the benefits of coaching and more people in the organization wanted this highly sought-after opportunity.

An intentional strategy for developing leaders as coaches was the natural next step in our ability to cast a wider coaching net. We knew we had earned the sponsorship, from the executive leaders, that would be needed to drive the coaching culture further into the organization via their own positive coaching experience. Their willingness to champion and support this next phase of the cultural shift was the lift the organization needed to begin the cascade of the coaching culture.

In thinking about how to structure this cascade we saw a clear need for two different but related approaches. We knew we would retain the executive coaching program described above for senior leaders in high-impact positions based on the size or scope of their responsibility. But this approach is time- and resource-intensive and therefore not scalable to a large number of managers. The second approach, introduced incrementally, involved developing managers to be more effective coaches—a strategy we called Coaching with Impact[9] (CWI). We wanted to create an economical approach for ensuring that all team members could benefit from effective coaching focused on achieving success in their respective roles and continuing to develop professionally. Building on the original premise of Leading with Impact—Know Yourself, Know Others—we added the additional concept Earn the Right to Coach. This idea of adapting your approach as a leader to the needs of others is supported by Krazmien and Berger (1997)[10] in their paper, "The Coaching Paradox," which describes the higher demands on the manager-employee relationship in today's competitive business environment, and the shift from managers controlling to empowering their employees.

In Coaching with Impact we added the DiSC[11] and Motivator assessment tools to build on the 360 feedback participants had received through the prerequisite Leading with Impact. The DiSC and Motivator tools were added to teach the concept that there are individual differences in communication styles and motivations that may lead to frustration for leaders and their employees alike unless the impact of these differences is understood. When leaders adapt their style to the preferences of others, their effectiveness as communicators is enhanced.

Prior to the CWI seminar, each participant is assigned an internal coach, drawn from a broader leadership development cadre within Wells Fargo, who provides coaching based on the participant/client's 360 feedback and the DiSC and Motivator data and follows up with the participant as long and as frequently as the coach and client deem necessary for the client to feel confident and effective as a manager-coach.

Day 1 of the two-day Coaching with Impact seminar is devoted to teaching two concepts:

- **Determine the Right Approach** is about learning to untangle the differences between coaching and performance management. As a manager expected to do both, the skill is to engage in performance management when the team member is not meeting goals, and coaching when the individual is meeting expectations, has the desire and potential to be even more effective, and views his or her manager as a trusted mentor.

- **Earn the Right to Coach** involves understanding the arc that occurs in a managerial relationship, from setting expectations and holding employees accountable to being perceived as a trusted mentor. Clarity about the current nature of the manager and employee's relationship is fundamental to being able to advance into a coaching role.

On Day 2, CWI participants practice coaching. In groups of three or four, they engage in videotaped role-play, holding both performance management and coaching conversations. They receive in-the-moment feedback, evaluate themselves, and receive constructive comments from their peers and coach. Participants then continue to receive individual coaching until they have gained traction in the coach aspect of their managerial role.

As a macro strategy, Coaching with Impact was offered in a cascade beginning with the most senior managers, who were held accountable by Mr. B for their individual development plans, and who in turn held their next level managers accountable following participation in the course, and so on. Unlike the Leading with Impact seminar, which began by bringing together managers who didn't work together day-to-day, CWI was ultimately offered to intact vertical management teams with the intent of creating shared coaching language and concepts that would become an integral part of team planning and discussion.

SUMMARY AND RECOMMENDATIONS

This case study has focused on the experience of one organization over roughly a decade. It is informed by the research and writings of others on the topic of coaching in an organizational context. Based on our reading and our experience, we assert that developing and sustaining a coaching culture within any organization requires time, executive support, and a thoughtful strategy aligned with the business strategy. The key organizational variables to consider, based on the Columbia Coaching Certification Program's framework for the individual coaching process, are:[12]

- **High Standards**: The presence of trust and ethical conduct in which there is absolute clarity about and clear boundaries around what it means to be offered or engaged in a coaching process within the organizational context.

- **Agenda**: Answers the question: Why do we need, or want, a coaching culture? What's the compelling business need?

- **Earn the Right**: Just as an individual coach must earn the right to engage and progress with a coaching client, the organization must also be seen as credible with regard to coaching practices. At minimum the organization is one in which

» Learning is valued.

» Relationships are valued.

» Seeking and receiving feedback is the norm.

- **Involvement:** Involvement of leaders as role models, involvement of employees with their leaders and their peers, and linkage of coaching to the business strategy.

We propose that the conditions needed to establish an effective coaching culture can provide a framework not only for designing a coaching culture, but for testing for the presence of an organizational culture that may be ready to introduce an internal coaching process.

We have begun to introduce the internal coaching strategies described in this case study to additional business divisions across Wells Fargo. In doing so, we seek to align executive coaching to each division's business strategy and organizational culture. Our next step will be to adapt specific interventions to best support the division's objectives as we look for ways to replicate the outcomes described in this case study.

NOTES

1. P. Hersey and K. H. Blanchard, "Life Cycle Theory of Leadership," *Training and Development Journal* 23, no. 5 (1969): 26–34.

2. Advanced Leadership Seminar© 2002 Wells Fargo & Company. All rights reserved.

3. S. D. Baker, "Followership: The Theoretical Foundations of a Contemporary Construct," *Journal of Leadership and Organizational Studies* 14 (2007): 50–60.

4. Leading with Impact© 2004 Wells Fargo & Company. All rights reserved.

5. Acumen® Leadership WorkStyles™ (LWS), Human Synergistics International.

6. Speakeasy©. Communications Consulting, San Francisco, CA. All rights reserved.

7. M. Watkins, *The First 90 Days: Critical Success Strategies for New Leaders at All Levels* (Boston: Harvard Business Publishing, 2003).

8. *The Vision & Values of Wells Fargo*© 2012 Wells Fargo & Company. All rights reserved.

9. Coaching with Impact© 2005 Wells Fargo & Company. All rights reserved.

10. M. Krazmien and F. Berger, "The Coaching Paradox," *International Journal of Hospitality Management* 16, no. 1 (1997): 3–10.

11. DiSC® is a registered trademark of Inscape Publishing, Inc.

12. The authors have integrated the business strategy and organizational culture at Wells Fargo with the Columbia Coaching Certification Program's foundational guiding principles: adhere to high standards of ethical conduct; focus on the client's agenda; build commitment through involvement; and earn the right to advance at each stage of the coaching process. The Columbia Coaching Certification Program website, accessed February 11, 2014, http://www.tc.columbia.edu/coachingcertification/index.asp?Id=Coach+Foundations&Info=Coach+Foundations.

Patricia M. Armstrong is the managing director of family dynamics at Abbot Downing, a Wells Fargo business serving the needs of ultra-high-net-worth families and individuals, endowments, and foundations. Prior to her current role Pat was the head of human resources for the wealth management business of Wells Fargo. Pat holds a doctorate in counseling psychology from Southern Illinois University.

Stephanie Duignan is a senior vice president and manager of talent, diversity and organizational development at Wells Fargo in Wealth, Brokerage and Retirement; she manages the overall strategy for executive and leadership development initiatives, including succession planning, early talent planning, diversity and inclusion, organizational development, and executive coaching. Stephanie holds a master's degree in organizational psychology from the California School of Professional Psychology.

Denise P. Verolini is a senior vice president and the director of team member experience at Wells Fargo Private Bank. She partners with and provides support to a diverse group of cross-functional teams. Denise earned her doctorate in clinical psychology from the California School of Professional Psychology.

Nancy J. Amick is an organizational development consultant and executive coach at Wells Fargo in Wealth, Brokerage and Retirement. She holds a doctorate in clinical psychology from the California School of Professional Psychology.

Lorilee Mills is an organizational development consultant and executive coach at Wells Fargo in Wealth, Brokerage and Retirement, developing customized strategies for leaders and teams. Lorilee holds a bachelors degree in psychology from Iowa State University.

2

"Wszystko jest mozliwe" ("Everything is possible"): Coach Principled Leadership in Eastern Europe

Alan Polansky

Henry McGovern, a U.S. entrepreneur in his mid-twenties, went to Wroclaw, Poland, in the early '90s, shortly after Poland shook off the yoke of Communism. He was eager to build something; the timing was right. What could be more exciting than creating a Western business model in Poland, situated right in the middle of Central and Eastern Europe? Henry built AmRest, today a public company of more than 700 restaurants with sales of over $800 million in Poland, the Czech Republic, Bulgaria, Croatia, Slovakia, Hungary, Russia, the U.S., France, Spain, and China. As Henry struggled with a legion of obstacles to build his first Pizza Hut in Wroclaw, Poland in 1993, he quickly realized that no matter what he wanted to do he encountered the same response from the Poles: "Nie możliwe." ("Not possible.") Henry responded with "Wszystko jest możliwe" ("Everything is possible")—the AmRest motto for every challenge the organization has faced since its beginning.

Several years ago it became evident that to continue to grow effectively within the framework of our core values, AmRest had to adjust its leadership style. The historically embedded command and control style of leadership was not the best to consistently drive results and provide a strong and innovative leadership pipeline; this style was holding us back. Yet, in this part of the world, changing long-held behaviors was going to be a huge challenge. Enter Coach Principled Leadership! "Wszystko jest możliwe."

Today, more than 20,000 employees—2,000-plus managers—around the globe work for AmRest. Our franchised brands are household names; most are ranked either first or second worldwide in their respective market segments: Starbucks, KFC, Pizza Hut, Burger King, Applebee's (U.S.)[1] and La Tagliatella (Spain).

Our core values (see sidebar), linked inexorably to "Wszystko jest możliwe," have played a key role in creating AmRest's culture and sustaining our rapid and successful growth. Our commitment to people: to hire the best, to continually update their hard and soft skills, to encourage them to achieve stretch goals (another core value) . . . . In short, to help them be the best they can be.

AmRest Core Values

"We live them and constantly reaffirm them—they are front and center in our daily activities." - Henry McGovern

Customer Focus. *We listen and actively respond to our customers. Our decisions and actions are customer focused.*

Operational Excellence. *We have a passion for excellence. We push to be the best in the world. We have the energy and confidence to confront today's reality and make the changes necessary to be the best.*

Positive Energy. *We execute with enormous positive energy, and have the ability to invigorate others . . . we hate bureaucracy and all the nonsense that comes with it.*

Feedback. *We desire and believe in direct and honest feedback. Politics have no place in our company.*

Stretch Goals. *We know that nothing is impossible . . . set aggressive targets . . . recognize and reward progress, while understanding accountability and commitment.*

Commitment to People. *We believe in the intentions of our people and want them to take responsibility, develop and have fun.*

Accountability. *We do what we say, we are accountable, we act like owners.*

Profitability. *Profit, like breathing, is indispensable. Profit is not our sole goal, it is a means of achieving our opportunities.*

In 2010, in an effort to expand the quality and quantity of our leadership pipeline, AmRest introduced Coach Principled Leadership,[2] with the intention of instilling its concepts throughout our restaurant operations staff and our restaurant support team. In an environment with a long history of command and control leadership, with top-down authoritarian decision-making, we wanted to engage and empower a broader range of leaders who lived our core values and produced results. We believed that by providing senior and middle managers, and ultimately our restaurant managers, with the tools and training to be more collaborative leaders,[3] we could drive growth and profitability.

Our initial focus was to reduce command and control leadership, decrease turnover, and move toward becoming an Employer of Choice.

Command and Control Has Its Niche (a small one)

A few years after I joined AmRest, Henry McGovern asked me to go to Prague to run a recently purchased and deeply troubled KFC market. With only six restaurants, the market managed to lose $8 million during the three years prior to our purchase. There was very little right about what was going on in that distressed market.

Until then, I had given little thought to leadership style. Mine was a combination of collaboration and consensus, learned through experience. For example, as a deputy assistant secretary of commerce in the Nixon/Ford administration, I had chaired an interagency committee responsible for negotiating trade agreements that insured textile imports would not be disruptive to the U.S. textile industry. Needless to say, with the departments of Labor, State, the Treasury, and Commerce involved, along with keenly interested, sensitive, and powerful congressmen from southern textile-producing states, a command and control leadership style was not only counterproductive, it was out of the question.

Now, as we tried to build a profitable Czech KFC market, I realized I had to quickly make a number of tough decisions, especially about people. Using command and control leadership, I fired several store managers, introduced the Disciplined Operating System (DOS), and focused on getting the market profitable. With the help of Drew O'Malley, who ran the market the first year after acquisition, we turned the corner on profitability in just over a year. In the following seven years, under my leadership, the Czech market became one of the most profitable and successful KFC markets worldwide.

Collaboration for the Long Haul = Superior Results

After cleaning house in the Czech Republic using a command and control leadership style, I changed back to a more collaborative approach. To engage our people and stimulate them to perform at very high levels, it was important to listen to their ideas, ask them challenging questions, support them with my experience, and spend time with them during and after work hours. This approach built an exceptionally potent, high-performing team glued together by a strong bond of trust, and we accomplished numerous stretch goals. For example, we drove turnover from 250 percent to less than 100 percent in a little over one year. Our cash flow averaged more than 18 percent annually for several years, and every year we were one of the top two European markets with the highest customer satisfaction ratings. We increased the number of new restaurants by just under 35 percent every year for seven years. In 2001 Yum Brands named Czech KFC the most profitable market with the highest sales increase from 2000–2001 in the world. And finally, after buying a competitor, in six short weeks we renovated the restaurants and opened up eight KFCs in one weekend.

Through these early experiences at AmRest, I quickly learned that the command and control approach was necessary and had value when used appropriately but sparingly, and that collaborative leadership was an extremely effective way to motivate people to produce superior results continuously.

Building a Leadership Pipeline: AmRest University and Executive Coaching

After seven years as brand president for KFC in the Czech Republic, I returned to Wroclaw and started AmRest University in 2006. It was designed to develop our leadership pipeline by focusing on the development of high potentials. We wanted leaders who lived the core values and produced results. Our senior management team, led by our co-founder Henry McGovern, taught all courses. It was during this time that I began mentoring our young team, became interested in coaching, and decided to enroll in the Columbia Coaching Certification Program (CCCP) as a member of its first cohort. As a requirement of the CCCP practicum we had to coach fifty hours, a requirement I fulfilled coaching selected AmRest executives and managers.

In my one-on-one coaching at AmRest, I quickly discovered that somewhere between 70 and 80 percent of my clients were using command and control as their sole leadership style. This approach was preventing many of them from achieving peak performance. During my initial year of executive coaching with AmRest senior execs, I saw the destructive impact of command and control leadership. Several departments lost numerous meritorious employees because of poor command and control leadership and solo decision-making, costing the company substantial sums of money. Over time it became obvious that command and control was not the leadership approach needed to drive results at AmRest.

We had to change, yet one element we were facing then, which continues to be an imposing obstacle now, is the geographic and historical background that influences Central and Eastern Europe. This became clear to me via my early coaching experience with leaders having a tough time changing away from command and control. One of my coaching clients told me, "My parents used command and control, my schools used it, the army certainly did, my first job was with a German company and they used it . . . . It's the only approach I know." This top-down authoritarian decision-making is the most prevalent style of leadership in Central Europe and throughout Western Europe. Yet, we knew if AmRest was to continue to grow effectively, we needed to reduce the command and control leadership and increase collaborative leadership. In this part of the world it was going to be a huge challenge.

COACH PRINCIPLED LEADERSHIP TRAINING

I convinced Henry McGovern and the executive management team that we had to make a change away from command and control. I worked with Dr. Anne Power, whom I had met at Columbia, to develop a training program using her Coach Principled Leadership methodology adapted to AmRest's needs. Our executive team agreed we should introduce Coach Principled Leadership to all executives and senior managers.

EXECUTIVE TRAINING

Anne Power and her Columbia Coaching Certification Program colleague John Schuster traveled to Wroclaw in February 2010 to run the training, with my assistance, for our top managers. There would be intensive in-person training, with periodic followup by telephone. The program emphasized coaching skills and principles for leaders to use in their relationships with others: listening, questioning, presence, and self-awareness. Our executive team, including our CEO Henry McGovern, attended a two-day session. Senior managers attended a three-day session. That week more than thirty executives received training in Coach Principled Leadership.

At the outset, we talked about the benefits of the coaching approach, underlining that we didn't expect the participants to become coaches, but to use the basic coaching approach to become more effective leaders. We wanted the participants to go out and practice not what they learned in a lecture, but what they experienced in the one-on-one coaching sessions. We used the fishbowl technique to help participants learn coaching skills through the experience of peer coaching: one person would select a workplace issue and then, using the newly learned coaching techniques, one of his or her peers would try to help resolve it. The other participants watched and provided feedback at the end of the session, as Anne, John, and I provided support.

POST-TRAINING FOLLOWUP

After the week of presentations and practice for the execs and the senior managers, we had a followup period. We asked each executive to select one or two people who didn't report to them and, using the Coach Principled Leadership format that we provided during the training, work with the selected employees on their challenges. Our followup approach was simple. Anne and I met with members of the executive group in an hour-long monthly conference call for four or five months. Each participant on the call shared good and bad experiences, challenges that came up, and how they handled them. We then discussed our individual experiences and how we overcame similar problems, a process that yielded engaging and forceful stories.

One exec, Director of Development Douglas Noble, said that in the past, when a direct report came to him with a problem, he would simply solve it for the employee, since it was fast and he had the experience. Doug admitted however that he would always have to follow up to make sure it got done the way he suggested. Now, he said, "I don't answer most questions but ask a question instead. I push the burden on the direct report's shoulders to come up with the answer. I'm there to help but it is the report's responsibility to figure out how it ought to be done consistent with our goals and core values." Doug also mentioned that his work/life balance had improved a great deal. This turned out to be a common experience, because the Coach Principled Leadership participants were effectively able to make their direct reports the owners of the solution to a problem. As a consequence they didn't have to keep notes regarding what was going on, nor follow up on the many details that were now the province of the direct report. The execs had more time to think strategically, look at the broader picture, and spend more time not only with family but helping their people develop and grow; in short, to be more complete leaders with time to invest in developing new leaders.

Mark Chandler, our worldwide CFO, said of his experience: "Coach Principled Leadership has been a game changer in the development of my team . . . . We have all been in coaching and the results have been nothing short of amazing. I personally learned the key difference between being a mentor and being a coach, which allowed me to be a more effective leader."

I repeated the same telephone followup format, plus face-to-face meetings, for the remaining senior managers who attended the initial three-day training session. These included brand presidents and district coaches (responsible for approximately forty-five restaurants). A majority of these operations senior managers reported that they felt an impact in performance improvements with direct reports and in their work/life balance. As a result, there was enough positive feedback to support the implementation of Coach Principled Leadership deeper into the system to ensure more people were using its principles.

COACH PRINCIPLED LEADERSHIP FOR AREA COACHES

We needed to cascade Coach Principled Leadership to all fifty-five of our area coaches, who each had approximately eight restaurants reporting to them. The challenge was to 1) simplify the program so it was easier to understand; 2) find a way to get managers to use it; and 3) develop an effective followup system for that many people.

Thanks to the sponsorship of Drew O'Malley, who was COO (now the CEO) of all AmRest brands in Central and Eastern Europe at that time, we introduced Coach Principled Leadership into our Disciplined Operating Systems structure. We use DOS Plus as the key operational yardstick to measure our performance against our goals. All managers in each store have an area of responsibility: general manager for sales and customers; assistant manager for people; shift manager for product, and another shift manager for facilities. The area coach conducts these store-level DOS Plus business reviews every month. The most effective area coaches were already using collaborative management techniques in the two- to three-hour review. The challenge was how to get more of the area coaches in all the brands to do the same, thereby improving performance and developing leaders more quickly.

Drew decided to review the principles and practices of DOS Plus throughout all our brands and at the same time introduce Coach Principled Leadership as a new initiative. The intent was to use Coach Principled Leadership as part of the monthly DOS Plus review. A video was made to illustrate this, with Drew playing the area coach conducting the DOS Plus review. In one case he conducted the review in a very command and control fashion (actually, as we'll see, quite representative of the way many area coaches did it). In the second case he did the review in a collaborative way using Coach Principled Leadership. What an eye-opener! When asked which they preferred, the area coaches unanimously chose the collaborative approach. When asked which approach represented daily life, close to 70 percent said, "Command and control."

Next, we simplified the approach to focus on listening, asking open-ended questions, getting clarity, creating an action plan, and a developing a win/win environment. Finally, we practiced the fishbowl technique that we used for the exec and senior manager training, along with other exercises. One impactful exercise, The Circle, involves using the Q-storming technique,[4] in which one participant describes a situation he or she needs help with, what he or she wants to achieve, and what solutions have already been tried. The other group members then ask questions to help the participant think differently about the situation in order to arrive at a solution. The moderator writes the questions on a flip chart. The participant listens to all the questions without responding—a very hard thing to do, and a good listening practice. Questions continue until the participant says stop and admits that he or she has a good idea about what to do about the challenge. The moderator asks the participant to rate the quality of the questions (scale 1–10) in regard to how helpful they were in reaching a solution. The moderator puts a score next to each question. All discuss each question as appropriate and a copy of the questions and ranking is given to all participants.

The challenge of the followup sessions was monumental. How do you institutionalize a leadership approach that most people agree is highly desirable but which, in practice, is not generally used, especially in Central and Eastern Europe? Herculean effort and the patience of Job come quickly to mind.

We decided the followup for all the brands would be similar to the followup for the executives and senior managers. It involved monthly sessions that would explore issues, problems, and success stories, and exercises whenever all participants were physically together. We had thirty-three area coaches for KFC, eight for Pizza Hut, six for Burger King, eight for Starbucks. We also had to train and provide followup for more than twenty area coaches, district coaches, and restaurant support staff for our Applebee's brand in the States. With Applebee's, I had the help of one of our district coaches from the Czech Republic, Libor Hubik, a certified coach who has used Coach Principled Leadership extensively and is totally committed to it. For the followup task within Central and Eastern Europe, I was fortunate to work with Oksana Staniszewska, another certified coach and fervent believer in Coach Principled Leadership, who at the time led our Training, Recruitment and Development department.

In our followup sessions with the area coaches, we discovered a number of interesting insights. For example, several participants admitted they first experimented with the Coach Principled Leadership collaborative approach at home—the reason being they were afraid to try it at work, since people were likely to ask, "What's the matter with you? You've always run this operation like a drill sergeant!"

Over and over, participants confirmed that the single biggest challenge of the Coach Principled Leadership training was learning to listen. Most people simply don't listen, thus failing to utilize a powerful tool that makes others feel important and comfortable and encourages dialogue. Effective listening sends the message, "I care about you and your ideas." Who wouldn't want to work for a boss who listens well?

As participants began to try out their new skills, stories illustrating the power of Coach Principled Leadership emerged. An area coach in a major Polish market fired a general manager who was running a store into the ground: sales were down, costs were up, and employee morale was shaky. The area coach decided to help the new manager get a quick start. He'd been close to the situation and knew it well, so he devised a plan of action focused on increasing sales and renewed effort on efficiency to reduce cost of sales. After a month in the store, however, the new manager told the area coach that she didn't want to carry out his plan, that she had devised a plan of her own. He was surprised. Without Coach Principled Leadership training, he said, he would have patted the manager on the shoulder and insisted he knew best. Instead, he listened and said okay. The manager's idea was to get back to basics across the board and renew pride in operational excellence—one of our core values. She proceeded to get the right people on the bus and in the right seats by firing several people—and the store turned around very quickly by virtually every measure. In retrospect, listening to her and not insisting on his way proved to be the right choice.

One of our general managers told how he was having a difficult time with an assistant manager who appeared to have a lot of promise but kept banging into the proverbial brick wall. After repeated attempts to help, the general manager had tentatively decided to fire the recalcitrant assistant, but then, in a final salvage attempt, sat him down and asked what he thought he, the general manager, should do. The assistant reluctantly told the manager that there were two other general managers whom he valued and who, he believed, could help him with sales and an inventory issue he was struggling with. Instead of being angered by this request, the general manager arranged for the assistant manager to receive training with the other general managers. The assistant manager caught fire, flourished, and in several months passed his boards for the general manager position.

Coach Principled Leadership had an impact at the administrative offices too. An HR manager responsible for hiring shared with me how she typically would conduct telephone interviews with several candidates for a position, generally inviting as many as three or four for on-site interviews, because when she felt unsure of a candidate over the phone she was unwilling to dismiss him or her solely on that basis, wanting instead to give the candidate the benefit of a personal interview. After exposure to Coach Principled Leadership, however, she practiced listening very intently and reported that lately she had needed to bring in only one or two candidates, thereby saving time and money. What happened, I asked. "In all cases, the people that I probably would have invited to come in for an interview simply talked their way out of it. In the face of my intent listening, they said way more than was needed."

These are but a few of dozens of stories that support the success of Coach Principled Leadership in increasing profitability and supporting leadership growth, especially of area coaches, by providing more time for them to reflect and to develop people.

RESULTS

At the outset we stated that we wanted to increase the collaborative approach versus the command and control style of leadership, reduce turnover, and move toward becoming an Employer of Choice. The stories our employees tell us are evidence we've made progress toward achieving each of these. We see dozens of examples of success in all brands and in all countries regarding people development, rotation, sales, operations, and profitability, with more time to spend on leadership and strategic thinking. Additionally, results from a recent survey show the command and control leadership style has decreased from approximately 70 percent to around 40 percent. A majority of our leaders are more collaborative now as a result of the shift toward Coach Principled Leadership. Our rotation has stabilized at 73 percent the past two years and in 2013 we became an Employer of Choice.

We also have specific examples of how Coach Principled Leadership is working to increase sales and profitability. In the Czech KFC market led by district coach Libor Hubik, where I've been doing Coach Principled Leadership team coaching, profitability increased 16 percent between 2011 and 2012. Most importantly, the engagement, high positive energy, accountability, and leadership of the entire team have been spectacular.

Another example is Pizza Hut in Poland. In 2012 there was a robust 17 percent improvement in Employer of Choice engagement scores, turnover decreased 20 percent, and sales increased 5 percent over 2011, leading Damian Rybak, Pizza Hut Poland's acting Brand President, to say, "Coach Principled Leadership has had a crucial influence on our business approach by stimulating open-minded thinking, which has been the base for our success. It has provided individual and overall people development, which has helped us achieve breakthrough results."

And finally, Alan Honan, a big Coach Principled Leadership supporter who runs the KFC market in Hungary, has produced some eye-popping results: profits were up 42 percent in 2012 over 2011. As Alan put it, "Coach Principled Leadership is simple, empowering, explainable and teachable. There are those rare occasions when we as leaders need to be directive; for everything else there is Coach Principled Leadership."

FURTHER ROLLOUT

Our next step in 2012 and 2013 was to provide further training to district coaches and area coaches, sharpening their Coach Principled Leadership awareness and skill set, and certifying those who qualify as ambassadors of the Coach Principled Leadership approach. So far all our district coaches and over 90 percent of the area coaches have been certified. These ambassadors will now work with our restaurant general managers, persuading them to use Coach Principled Leadership as part of their leadership style on a daily basis. In this way, we'll be able to trace more accurately, store by store, region by region, brand by brand, the results of Coach Principled Leadership, not only in increased profitability, but in reduced turnover and in greater achievement of Employer of Choice standards.

We will also introduce Coach Principled Leadership to our restaurant support staff in 2014. Mark Chandler, AmRest's worldwide CFO, a strong supporter and practitioner of Coach Principled Leadership, has taken the initiative to involve a vital part of our administrative staff in the Coach Principled Leadership experience.

We want our certified managers to have the same professionalism and pride that General Electric achieved with its Six Sigma Black Belts. We expect our managers to continue using Coach Principled Leadership in DOS Plus and to expand this approach to include job performance appraisals, one-on-one leadership coaching of employees identified as high potentials, area coach meetings, and the implementation of major initiatives such as lean management.

Although, as I wrote earlier, this whole process will take the strength of Hercules and the patience of Job, I'm convinced it is the only way we at AmRest can ensure that our ambitious growth goals can be achieved consistent with our core values. We need to grow with people who can think independently, who take the initiative, who value people and can build a bond of trust with them, who are happy to come to work every day and have a chance to be productive, who feel needed and appreciated, who want to be associated with the very best. Our experience has shown us that the most effective way to do this is to engage and empower people every single day through Coach Principled Leadership.

NOTES

1. Applebee's was sold in October 2012 and is no longer part of AmRest.

2. Coach Principled Leadership™ was developed in 2008 by Dr. Anne Power with Marsha Borling, Michael Cassatly, and Jane Taylor in response to the need to integrate a leadership coaching mindset and skillset in the health care environment. In 2010 Anne Power and Alan Polansky adapted Coach Principled Leadership to fit the needs at AmRest. Coach Principled Leadership uses the powerful tools of coaching to help leaders effectively lead, managers effectively manage, and teams and individuals effectively perform, innovate, and adapt to ever-changing realities (coachprincipledleadership.com).

3. We believe collaborative leadership involves engaging and empowering direct reports to produce results by building an atmosphere of trust.

4. Adapted from Marilee Adams, *Change Your Question Change Your Life*, 2nd ed. (San Francisco: Berrett-Koehler Publishers, 2009).

Alan J. Polansky is an executive coach at AmRest, a multibrand, multinational restaurant company headquartered in Wroclaw, Poland. Previously, Alan ran the Pizza Hut and KFC operations in Poland and was the brand president for KFC in the Czech Republic for several years. He founded and teaches at AmRest University. Alan initiated and continues to lead the implementation of Coach Principled Leadership with leaders, managers, and supervisors organization-wide. He holds a BA from Case Western Reserve University, an MA from the Nitze School of Advanced International

Studies at Johns Hopkins University, and a JD from the University of Michigan Law School.

3

Team Coaching in Health Care

Marsha Borling

There's an old saying that's applicable in healthcare today: "Change is a lot like heaven—it's great once you get there, but going is the hard part." Few disagree the healthcare industry must reinvent itself, and many believe the end result will be much better than today's system—but how to get there continues to generate anxious debate nationwide. Healthcare leaders are experiencing change unlike any they have known.

A journey through unprecedented change is fraught with new risks and demands talented individual leaders, as well as high-performing, adaptable leadership teams. However, in years past, most of the leadership development in healthcare focused on individuals, not teams. As more healthcare executives realize the need to elevate team performance, the opportunities for team coaching will increase. This chapter describes a successful and practical approach to team coaching, illustrated with actual client experience. While my main experience and current practice is within the healthcare industry, the principles and processes described here are applicable in virtually every field.

The team coaching process I use is adapted from the Columbia Coaching Certification Program coaching model I came to know well as a member of CCCP Cohort II. My adaptation includes these five phases:

1. Connecting with the team
2. Understanding the team's context
3. Establishing the team coaching goals
4. Contributing to the team's development and performance
5. Measuring team success

PHASE ONE: CONNECTING WITH THE TEAM

Connecting well with a new coaching client is essential. Connecting well with a team is just as essential, but more complex, because the coach must identify and connect with a team champion, in addition to the first contact person. Also, the coach must connect not only with the group as a whole, but also with the individual members of the group.

IDENTIFYING THE TEAM CHAMPION

Connecting with the "right" team champion is the first challenge of team coaching. Obviously, connecting with the first contact person from the team is important to make the sale, but often that first contact cannot or should not be the champion. Often the initial request for team coaching comes through the top Human Resources executive, on behalf of the CEO and his/her team. The HR executive is the logical contact person, given that leadership development is a critical HR function, and the HR executive is more likely to recognize the need for team coaching before anyone else on the team does. However, while connecting with the HR executive is important, the actual team development work must be owned and championed by the CEO. Reaching out, connecting, and ensuring that the CEO is the champion of the engagement is an added challenge specific to team coaching.

Thus, the first challenge for the coach is a political one: connecting well with the HR executive and partnering with him/her to launch the engagement, while connecting as soon as possible with the CEO. It must be made clear from the beginning that the CEO is the real leader of the team development work. Without the CEO engaged as the visible champion for the effort, the team's progress will be slow at best.

In my early work with teams, I intuitively knew this to be true, but my experience with one medical center (referred to here simply as "General Medical Center") drove that point home. It was clear at the start of the engagement with General Medical Center that some team members had convinced the CEO the executive team needed the help of a coach. He agreed to go along with the team development work—but delegated the engagement to the senior HR executive. While I knew this was not the ideal approach, I was optimistic that we could make it work. For the first four months, my communication liaison with the team was the HR executive. The CEO participated and seemed outwardly supportive; however, he was never the visible champion of the work. The other executive team members took their cue from the CEO, concluding that this was HR's project, and could therefore be treated as a softer, lower priority than other work the CEO promoted. Not surprisingly, our early progress was painfully slow and sporadic. At the end of that period, I met with the CEO and did what I should have done from the start (and now do as a matter of course): communicated clear expectations about the need for the CEO to own and promote the effort with the team.

Specifically, the CEO clearly conveyed (in words and behaviors) that the team work was a priority. During the second six months of the General Medical Center engagement, the CEO was true to his word, leading the effort with genuine commitment. The difference in the team's level of engagement was striking. As a result of this experience, I continue this practice in all my coaching engagements, asking to meet with the CEO privately before and/or after each team coaching session, and channeling all communication to the team through the CEO.

CONNECTING WITH THE GROUP AND INDIVIDUAL TEAM MEMBERS

Similar to individual coaching relationships, establishing credibility and trust is an important early step when coaching a team. The challenge with team coaching is that connection must be made with each individual team member, as well as with the team as a whole. With that in mind, I begin every team coaching engagement by meeting with the team members for one-on-one conversations. The objectives of these initial individual coaching conversations are to:

- Learn each member's views of the team's strengths/weaknesses

- Identify what each member wants from the team engagement

- Understand how each member believes she or he "fits in" and can contribute to the team's success

Prepared with this information, I am able to focus and customize the coaching sessions right from the start. For General Medical Center, the initial one-on-one conversations helped to keep team members engaged and committed to the effort, despite the initial lack of leadership from the CEO. Because I had built a relationship with each team member, they were able to evaluate the credibility of the engagement without the filter of the HR executive.

PHASE TWO: UNDERSTANDING THE TEAM'S CONTEXT

Discovering the team's desired vision and then comparing it to the team's current state is a worthy investment of upfront time. The insights gained during this phase are critical to frame and focus the coaching engagement. And when the context is accurately described, the coach is able to see any disconnects as they arise during the subsequent goal setting and coaching sessions.

DESCRIBING THE DESIRED FUTURE STATE

Most executives have participated in both poorly functioning and high-performing teams at some point in their careers. As a result they have assumptions about how a team should operate. Thus, one priority at the first coaching session is to help members surface their assumptions and decide together what type of team they want to be. Initially, the General Medical Center executives asked me to provide "canned" information describing high-performing teams, which they thought would save time, but the information was met with lukewarm interest.

Sensing the lack of enthusiasm, I put the information aside and facilitated the team through their "gut-level" descriptions of an ideal team, which helped surface the assumptions they were holding about how a team should perform. One method I often use to do this is to divide the team into small groups of three or four and give each group two sheets of paper and several markers. I instruct the groups to work together to draw a picture of an ideal, high-performing team on one sheet of paper, and a picture of the current team on the other. They must use pictures only, and not write any words on the paper. Without the constraints of seeking precise words, the members are able to express deeper and stronger feelings about the type of team they want to be. As each group describes its drawings to the whole team, key themes typically begin to emerge. The coach's role during the debrief is to help surface and "headline" each small group's thoughts and value statements about high-performing teams. The end result is a combined team vision members truly embrace.

DESCRIBING THE TEAM'S CURRENT STATE

Once the vision for the team is defined, the next step is to describe the team's current state. To help the team get a clear picture of its current performance I share the qualitative information gathered during the initial individual conversations (keeping it anonymous), as well as quantitative information from two team assessment tools (one measuring team trust behaviors, and another evaluating the team's performance across seven dimensions). The assessment results help quantify the team's strengths and weaknesses, and establish a baseline of measurable indicators to evaluate progress during the coaching engagement. The richer information, however, comes from my conversations with individual members, which give me a good understanding of the team's current strengths/weaknesses. When sharing the interview and team assessment information, I primarily use guided reflection and feedback to help the group collectively recognize the team's current state.

PHASE THREE: ESTABLISHING THE COACHING GOALS

The co-creation of clear coaching goals focuses the coaching engagement, and makes the measurement of progress feasible. Relevant coaching goals emerge from the gaps between the team's desired and current state. Exploring the gaps to identify impactful team goals is a critical step. Most teams need help with this, because exploring team weaknesses in an open way can be a challenge, especially when discussing uncomfortable subjects is not a team norm.

The General Medical Center team's desired future and current state showed a clear gap related to the group's ability to engage in conversations involving dissent; i.e., the team would politely nod and agree when together, and the real conversations would happen between two or three members in the "meeting after the meeting." Yet when the time came to set team developmental goals, the members initially avoided identifying the need to work on their ability to debate, disagree, and have the difficult conversations a high-performing team must have. Using provocative questions, reflection, and challenging the team's disconnect, I was able to help the group openly explore the gaps between desired and current state, and guide them in identifying and prioritizing the goals that matter most to their future performance.

PHASE FOUR: CONTRIBUTING TO THE TEAM'S SUCCESS

Once the coaching goals have been set, regular individual and group coaching sessions contribute to the team's success. While every coaching engagement is customized to meet team needs, the coaching plan I use includes team sessions augmented by individual sessions. A typical engagement would include

- Two-hour team coaching sessions monthly for the first three months, then every other month for six months (total six sessions), and

- One-hour individual coaching sessions monthly with each team member for the first three months, then every other month for six months (total six individual coaching sessions with each team member)

For busy executive teams, it's important to schedule all the team and individual coaching sessions at the beginning of the engagement. It works much better to lock calendars in advance rather than trying to schedule month to month.

COACHING THE INDIVIDUAL TEAM MEMBERS

The focus of individual coaching sessions is for the coach to help each team member privately explore his or her contribution to the team's ability to achieve its goals. These individual sessions can easily evolve into broader coaching conversations about issues that matter to the individual, and have nothing to do with the team's performance. While some tangential coaching is understandable and helps strengthen the connection between the coach and the individual, the coach should ensure the coaching stays focused on the individual's contribution to the team.

To help guide the individual sessions, I use a tool to gather and compile anonymous feedback from each team member about each of the others. The format is simple: "It would help us function more effectively as a team if you would do more of these behaviors, do less of these behaviors, and keep doing these behaviors." I use the tool early in the process, so during the second round of individual sessions, I communicate each member's feedback and help the individual create one or two personal goals that describe how she or he will help the team achieve its goals.

The focus of all subsequent individual coaching sessions is helping individual members contribute to the team's development, and gathering individual perceptions of team progress throughout the coaching phase.

COACHING THE GROUP

Team sessions can easily be sidetracked by unexpected organizational changes or challenges that take the group off course. In spite of this the coach's role is to help the team stay focused on its goals, or the desired outcomes cannot be achieved.

The format for each of the team coaching sessions includes:

- Check-in

- Review of action commitments and what has changed/not changed since last session

- Structured activities and group learning to advance team goals

- An activity to build team relations and communication

- Closing "circle of voices" (one takeaway, one commitment)

PHASE FIVE: MONITORING/MEASURING THE TEAM'S PROGRESS

The final phase, measuring the team's progress toward its goals, is very important to a successful outcome. A team that feels and sees measurable progress is buoyed by success and more likely to stay on course. It is the coach's job to hold the team accountable to insure this happens. I usually benchmark the success of a team coaching engagement in four ways:

1. During each of the individual coaching sessions, I use part of the coaching conversation to do a team member progress check. These progress checks help me to stay in tune with the team members' perceptions of what's working/not

working, how they are feeling about the work we are doing, and allow me to make adjustments as needed. I use this measure to continually re-focus and adjust the work I am doing with the team as a whole.

2.	At the start of each team session, I facilitate a "team progress check-in" for the group to discuss together how well they met the action commitments from the last session. While I already have a fairly clear idea of how well the team is doing based on the individual check-ins, having the group discuss their progress (or lack of progress) together helps to move the group forward and break through barriers.

3.	At the end of six and twelve months, I usually encourage teams to repeat the trust behaviors and team performance tools. Many teams want a quantitative measure that they can continue to use to track their progress over time, and these easy-to-use tools fill that need.

4.	At the final team coaching session, I use half of the session to facilitate a group reflection on where they started and where they are now. Together, we also identify the remaining work, and reach consensus regarding how the team will "hold the gain" going forward.

As I continue to work with teams, I am certain I will find new practices to incorporate into this five-phase process. Each team is different and I learn enormously from each. With that in mind I am grateful for the opportunities I am afforded working with the dedicated individuals in health care who give extra time and commitment to serving on leadership teams.

———

Marsha Borling is a healthcare management consultant and executive coach. Her firm, Borling + Associates, Ltd., focuses on executive coaching for healthcare administrative and physician leaders, leadership team development and coaching, medical staff and governing board relations. Marsha holds an MA in Management Communications.

4

The Internal Coaching Process at Wells Fargo Wealth Management

Patricia M. Armstrong, Nancy J. Amick, Stephanie Duignan,
Lorilee M. Mills, and Denise P. Verolini

ALIGNMENT WITH BUSINESS GOALS

At the Wells Fargo wealth management group, the purpose of the internal coaching practice is to help leaders increase their effectiveness at managing by influence, achieving results, and growing the business. Most of the coaching engagements focus on executive transitions in which the coaching goals include ensuring that the leader successfully assimilates into his or her new role, quickly learning how to positively influence others at this executive level. Goals also include avoiding common new leader pitfalls such as neglecting to align leadership behaviors with the needs of the current environment or taking actions that are incongruent with the organizational culture.

COACHING PHILOSOPHY

Wealth management's coaches work from a consistent methodology grounded in the business model and business strategies of the leader being coached. The coach's role is to be an objective, strategic business partner in a one-to-one relationship built on trust. The coach and client establish specific and observable coaching goals to help the client increase his or her skills and effectiveness to deliver business results. The coaching engagement includes the client's direct manager and human resources partner, who work together with the client and coach to help set the coaching goals and provide feedback on progress toward the established goals throughout the coaching engagement.

The coach also provides coaching to the client's manager so that he or she can lead and coach the client to the highest level of effectiveness. To develop trust, the details of all coaching conversations remain confidential between coach and client. A formal coaching agreement clearly specifies the information that will be shared with the organization, the client's manager, and any other stakeholders identified at the beginning of the engagement. We believe that it is critical for the client to be fully aware of, and agree to, the limits of confidentiality before coaching begins.

INTERNAL EXECUTIVE COACH SELECTION AND DEVELOPMENT

The recruitment of internal coaches possessing the requisite skills, integrity, credibility, and ability to manage their dual clients—the leader and the organization—is arguably the most important task in establishing a viable internal coaching practice. At wealth management, coach selection is shared by the leadership development and executive coaching practice leader, the business head executive sponsor, and the human resources leader. Our selection criteria specify that a coach:

- Understands the business vision, strategy, business model, and business drivers

- Effectively manages confidentiality under all circumstances

- Models leadership behaviors that are aligned with the vision and values of the organization

- Has personal credibility with senior leaders

- Effectively uses 360 feedback and other assessment instruments at the right time for the right reasons within the context of the coaching engagement

- Knows how to balance established coaching methodology and protocol with a tailored and customized approach

- Consults with master coaches to ensure high-quality and high-value work and to increase self-awareness in the role of coach

- Possesses strong facilitation skills with a range of audience sizes and a variety of leadership and team-building interventions

- Has an advanced degree in the behavioral and/or organizational sciences, is either certified or enrolled in a coaching certification program, and is committed to life-long learning

- Is well versed in executive coaching literature and practices, including executive transition, change management, and ROI research

In addition to these criteria, the internal coach is expected to demonstrate the following capabilities:

- A level of corporate experience to be able to understand the cultural, political, and developmental context of the senior leaders he or she will coach

- Prior internal consulting experience, including a demonstrated ability to effectively deal with potential conflicts of interest by serving the best interests of the client and the organization while also managing his or her own personal reputation and credibility

- Certification from or current enrollment in a professional coach training program. The coaches described in this case study completed the Columbia Coaching Certification Program at Columbia University.

- Certification in a variety of assessment tools that support the coaching process (such as Clifton StrengthsFinder, DiSC, Acumen, Extraordinary Leader, and other proprietary internal 360 tools)

- Ongoing skill development, which is essential as a way for the internal coach to model leadership development across the business unit. Personal developmental objectives are identified each year.

SELECTION AND USE OF EXTERNAL EXECUTIVE COACHES

Wells Fargo wealth management uses external executive coaches as a complementary strategy. The development of the group's internal executive coaching function reflects our fundamental view that there is inherent value in a coaching process deeply integrated into the organizational culture. But we also believe that an open architecture of both internal and external coaches provides a more comprehensive approach to our business leaders' diverse needs.

There will always be situations in which an external coach may be the better choice for a senior executive, based on factors such as personality fit, specialization, or the need to address the client's concerns about objectivity and confidentiality. In our experience the majority of internal clients readily see the advantage of working with an internal coach who understands their organizational culture, but having the flexibility to offer an external option as needed adds further credibility to the overall objectivity and transparency of the internal coaching function.

Prior to engaging an external coach, one or more members of the internal executive coaching team screen him or her for criteria such as:

- Experience working as a coach or manager within a large organization, defined as 10,000 or more employees

- Ability to integrate a business vision, strategy, and organizational culture with coaching methodology

- Understanding of the expectations associated with a coaching engagement that occurs within an organizational context, e.g. that there are multiple stakeholders and some explicit limits to confidentiality

- Recognition of the importance of working within both the organizational context and the executive's context

- Ability to clearly articulate how coaching results will be measured

- Understanding of how to put processes in place to ensure results will be sustained over time

- Modeling of the leadership behaviors that executives are expected to demonstrate

There are also some disqualifying factors we consider in screening external coaches:

- Lack of a structured approach or inability to articulate a method of coaching

- A "one size fits all" approach with no flexibility in tailoring methodology or timing of components for individual coaching situations

- Unwillingness to adapt his or her approach to the needs of the organization or the executive

- Any indication that ethical behavior is not highly valued

- Lack of personal and professional presence

- Inability to emulate the behavioral results desired in the executive to be coached

One final consideration of the open architecture model is that on occasion, an executive will ask to work with an external coach with whom he or she already has a relationship. We've given this a try and generally speaking it hasn't been effective. There is no substitute for the objectivity of a fresh engagement within the organizational context and based on independent data—as opposed to bringing a new organizational context into an existing coaching relationship that began under different circumstances. Our experience suggests that it is best to work with the client and the sponsoring organization together to select a coach who engenders both confidence and a sense of neutral objectivity for all parties to the engagement.

SELECTION AND FUNDING OF EXECUTIVE COACHING CLIENTS

Taking the time to define the purpose of and the approach for the internal coaching program helped us to define the desired executive coaching services as customized, high-impact leadership development solutions. In adopting the open architecture approach, we felt it was important to create the expectation that the selection of a coach, whether internal or external, would be cost-neutral. Therefore, we made the decision to charge the direct manager of each executive coaching client the prevailing market rate for external executive coaching services. The coaching fees are defined up front in the coaching engagement and contracting process; this way we can quickly assess the manager's commitment and avoid the possibility of cost clouding the selection of an internal versus an external resource. By keeping the choice cost-neutral, we are better able to focus on the fit of the coach's skill set in relation to the client and coaching objectives.

CONTRACTING AND GOAL SETTING

Considerable attention has been given to the importance of contracting and goal setting in establishing an effective coaching relationship.[1] When coaching is offered within an organizational context it is arguably even more important that clients understand the fundamentals of what coaching is and is not, what they can expect of the coach, and what is expected of them during the engagement. For example, it is useful to cover details such as how other internal clients typically use coaching and who brings the agenda to the coaching meeting.

The coach and client also need to come to agreement regarding the logistics of the engagement: how often they will meet; whether they will meet by phone, in person, or both; who else will be involved in the coaching process—always a critical discussion in an organizational setting—and the duration of the engagement.

For internal coaches who may engage with the client's manager, peers, and direct reports in a variety of contexts, talking with the client about how confidentiality will be handled is essential for establishing trust in the coaching relationship. It is helpful for clients to understand that the coach has multiple stakeholders and to have clarity about what information will be shared and with whom.

Setting coaching goals in the early phases of the engagement ensures that coach and client agree on the purpose of coaching and the desired outcomes. All coaching goals are then discussed in a joint meeting with the client's manager, the human resources partner, coach, and client to ensure that all who support the client are in alignment with the direction and purpose of coaching. Developing a written agreement between coach and client is an effective way to confirm the purpose and guidelines of the engagement.

STAKEHOLDER INVOLVEMENT

Identifying the stakeholders who have a vested interest in the client's success, then soliciting feedback regarding what they need from the client, is a key aspect of the internal coaching engagement. The requested feedback should include actionable ways the client can be a more effective boss, subordinate, or partner, and at minimum is gathered from the client's direct manager and their human resources partner, but it is often useful to get feedback from a wider range of stakeholders.

CUSTOM 360 ASSESSMENT

Customized 360 feedback is gathered in almost all of wealth management's coaching engagements as a way for clients to understand how they are perceived by others and whether they are effective in leading and managing their team and the business. If the client is new to his or her role and to the team, the 360 feedback is typically solicited after the client has been in the role for at least six months. For such new leader engagements, stakeholder interviews focus on business priorities and the associated expectations of the leader.

In the customized 360 process, the coach develops a set of questions, with input from the client, that are specific to the client's business and role. The coach then conducts 1:1 interviews with raters who have been selected by the client, the client's manager, and the coach. Data is aggregated, and feedback on the client's strengths and areas of development is outlined in a written report that is reviewed with the client. The client develops an action plan based on the feedback. Highlights from the 360 assessment are shared by the client in a joint meeting with his or her manager, human resources partner, and the coach. The coaching process then focuses on closing the gap between where the client is now and where he or she needs to be in order to function optimally.

IN-PERSON OBSERVATION

Throughout a coaching engagement, the coach observes the client in multiple settings, such as meetings with peers and business partners, and presentations to small and large audiences. This provides valuable opportunities to gain insight not only into how others respond to the client's words and actions, but into the people with whom and the business and culture in which the client works, so the coach is better able to calibrate the work to the situation.

For example, a coach may sit in on a client's team offsite to learn about their business opportunities and challenges, observe how the client shows up as a leader, and understand more about the people the client leads. Typically, during breaks the coach gives the client feedback about whether he or she is leading in a way that will help obtain the desired outcomes. A debrief following the meeting about what did and did not work helps the client develop and sustain the behaviors that lead to success.

Because clarity and transparency are key underpinnings of wealth management's coaching culture, the client introduces the coach to his or her team. Given our strong coaching culture, coaching from the internal leadership development team is typically viewed as recognition of the client's high potential and management's investment in his or her success. As a result, the coach is generally embraced by the team.

TEAM DEVELOPMENT

At the Wells Fargo wealth management group, we believe that a leader is only as strong as his or her team; therefore, when indicated, coaches also work with a client's team. Such work is created in conjunction with the client and is always done in a manner that gives the client opportunities to have high impact with his or her team. The goal is to help the client create a collaborative team that works together in the service of achieving success in the business. Team development tools typically used at wealth management include Team Effectiveness and Clifton StrengthsFinder.

TEAM EFFECTIVENESS

Team Effectiveness,[2] a process designed by wealth management's leadership development team, assists teams in working collaboratively to achieve optimal business results. It takes place in an offsite interactive meeting facilitated by the coach. Topics for discussion, identified by the client and his or her team, may include developing the team's vision and values and creating the working agreements that will lead to strong team performance. Typically, prior to the meeting, the coach conducts individual interviews with each person on the client's team to gather background and context and to ensure that the meeting reflects what the team most needs and wants to work on. When this process is integrated into the client's overall coaching engagement, it gives the coach an opportunity to model engagement behaviors as well as provide the client real-time feedback.

STRENGTHSFINDER

The Clifton StrengthsFinder[3] is sometimes used to assist individuals and teams in understanding their diverse talents and how to best leverage them to work effectively as a team. This process can be particularly useful not only when there's a new leader, but when the team is also fairly new to working together.

STRENGTHS AND IMPACT ASSOCIATED WITH AN INTERNAL COACHING PRACTICE

The benefits of internal coaching include providing the client a coach who knows the organization's culture and understands the political landscape in which the client works. An internal coach also has a practical understanding of the organization-specific leadership behaviors and actions that lead to success, or failure. When strong organizational and individual support is given to leadership development, the value of an internal coaching practice can be considerable.

In evaluating our own practice effectiveness, we surveyed thirty-one clients coached between 2004 and 2009; twenty individuals responded. Of those twenty respondents, between fifteen and seventeen agreed or strongly agreed with the following statements:

• The coaching I received improved my relationship with my boss.

• The coaching I received improved my relationship with my peers.

• The coaching I received improved my relationship with my partners.

- The coaching I received improved my relationship with my direct reports."

Some individual comments were:

- *Helped my boss and me agree on what success looks like and has helped me be more effective in how I communicate.*

- *Coaching helped me to see whether or not my own personal assessments of my peers were on target or not, and then how to make adjustments.*

- *While I've always been engaged with my partners, they are seeing me be more actively engaged—not afraid to speak up and share my opinion, whether they want to hear it or not.*

- *[With direct reports] is where I saw the greatest improvement. When my coach helped me get comfortable with myself and become a better coach and leader, my directs noticed a huge difference.*

Similarly, between sixteen and eighteen of the twenty respondents agreed or strongly agreed with the statements:

- My coach challenged my thinking.

- The coaching I received helped me make better business decisions.

- The coaching I received had a direct impact on the organization's business results.

Individual comments included:

- *[My coach] has allowed me to reflect on how communications are perceived, not just content.*

- *Even after the coaching, my coach remains the "voice on my shoulder."*

- *[The coaching] made me more focused on what it was important to accomplish and avoiding non-impactful noise.*

- *The coaching I received helped me make better "people" decisions, which often lead to better business decisions.*

- *I believe the coaching has helped me "quick start" and continue to exceed revenue goals year-to-date.*

- *Peer, partner and direct report interaction strongly impacts results. My growth in each of these areas definitely helped us exceed plan.*

Finally, when asked to respond to the statement, "I am a more effective leader today as a result of the coaching," nineteen respondents answered affirmatively.

One client described the experience as follows: "My coach was instrumental in helping me develop my strategy and drive culture change as I transitioned into my new role three years ago. [My coach] made me slow down in order to speed up the change and her probing questions made me more thoughtful and deliberate in my execution and communication strategy and I know prevented me from making costly mistakes. My coach's involvement as a coach and sounding board has been instrumental to my success."

CHALLENGES OF AN INTERNAL COACHING PRACTICE

The primary challenge faced by internal coaches is protecting the confidentiality among multiple stakeholders. Trust is an essential component of the coaching relationship—without it, there *is* no coaching relationship. The real work is accomplished when the client can be candid about successes and failures without fear of retribution or consequence. In an internal program coaches serve multiple stakeholders—the organization, the client's manager, and the client. How confidentiality is managed in the service of all requires a great deal of skill, forethought, and consultation.

As already discussed, under these circumstances it is essential for coaches to clarify at the beginning of an engagement what information will be communicated to management and why, and to seek ongoing professional consultation themselves to maintain clarity about appropriate boundaries. Sharing information with management about how to best coach the client around his or her areas of strength and challenge is essential—and is a key reason why internal coaching adds value—but any breach of the agreed-upon information-sharing protocol will quickly undermine the credibility of the entire function. Managers will test the coaches and the coaches must pass the test each time. An organization contemplating an internal coaching function must appreciate the significance of this issue and be willing to honor confidentiality rules. Coaches contemplating an internal role must be ever vigilant in this regard.

Notes

1. L. Whitworth, K. Kimsey-House, H. Kimsey-House and P. Sandahl, *Co-Active Coaching*, 2nd ed. (Mountain View, CA: Davies-Black Publishing, 2007).

2. Team Effectiveness© 2004 Wells Fargo & Company. All rights reserved.

3. Clifton StrengthsFinder© 2000 The Gallup Organization, Princeton, NJ.

Patricia M. Armstrong is the managing director of family dynamics at Abbot Downing, a Wells Fargo business serving the needs of ultra-high-net-worth families and individuals, endowments, and foundations. Prior to her current role Pat was the head of human resources for the wealth management business of Wells Fargo. Pat holds a doctorate in counseling psychology from Southern Illinois University.

Nancy J. Amick is an organizational development consultant and executive coach at Wells Fargo in Wealth, Brokerage and Retirement. She holds a doctorate in clinical psychology from the California School of Professional Psychology.

Stephanie Duignan is a senior vice president and manager of talent, diversity and organizational development at Wells Fargo in Wealth, Brokerage and Retirement; she manages the overall strategy for executive and leadership development initiatives, including succession planning, early talent planning, diversity and inclusion, organizational development, and executive coaching. Stephanie holds a master's degree in organizational psychology from the California School of Professional Psychology.

Lorilee Mills is an organizational development consultant and executive coach at Wells Fargo in Wealth, Brokerage and Retirement, developing customized strategies for leaders and teams. Lorilee holds a bachelors degree in psychology from Iowa State University.

Denise P. Verolini is a senior vice president and the director of team member experience at Wells Fargo Private Bank. She partners with and provides support to a diverse group of cross-functional teams. Denise earned her doctorate in clinical psychology from the California School of Professional Psychology.

5

External Coaches: Assessing an Organizational Client

Lou Chrostowski

External coaches are most effective when they work in partnership with their client organizations. The Executive Coaching Forum advocates creating a coaching partnership, establishing a win-win approach in which "all partners plan the process together, communicate openly, and work cooperatively toward the ultimate accomplishment of overarching organizational objectives."[1] In such a partnership, the coach works with the key stakeholders—the executive coaching client, Human Resources, and others within the organization—to ensure that the executive's learning, development, and behavioral change will support the organization's business needs and strategic objectives.

A great deal has been written about leadership development, talent management, and executive coaching. Generally this material is discussed from one of just two perspectives: either the organization's, or the coach's. The current literature targeted at organizations typically explores best practices, for example, in bringing coaching into an organization, or, in the case study presented in the chapter "Wells Fargo: The Evolution of a Coaching Culture," what's necessary to institute an organization-wide coaching initiative. Literature written for coaches focuses primarily on how to be an effective or successful coach.

My own interests, however, fall between those two most common perspectives. I write of the relationship between a coach and an organization. But first, some background is in order.

As the coaching profession has grown and evolved, so too, within the corporate organizational context, has the field of talent management. In the 1980s, personnel departments morphed into Human Resources, and organizations began to look more strategically at managing their people assets. This trend continued into the 1990s, and the strategic focus of Human Resources grew to encompass recruitment and retention; employee relations, rewards, and recognition; employee communications; organizational design; succession planning; and learning and development.

In the 2000s the field has become more holistic. A growing number of organizations have moved away from task-focused or reactive coaching, establishing instead organizational coaching capability linked to business needs, strategy, and culture, in which coaching addresses the developmental needs of senior executives and professionals. These are organizations with a clearly articulated vision that have made it a strategic initiative not only to identify the skills and behaviors necessary to achieve desired outcomes, but to create the environment to support them.

Over the course of thirty-three years, my career evolved from internal talent management to external coach, and then to a coaching program manager with Karlin Sloan & Company. I have worked both within and external to a number of organizations designing, implementing, and/or managing and assessing the success or value of coaching initiatives, and so have learned what to look for in a potential coaching engagement to ensure a maximum benefit to the coaching client.

In most instances I found the individual client willing and coachable and the client organization supportive. Yet, it was not unusual to find myself faced with a "good" client working in an organization inhospitable to coaching, thus limiting the odds of a successful coaching engagement. I began to identify themes critical to the effectiveness of coaching within an organization, and that determine whether coaching makes sense at all in certain organizations. These include:

- Business context and strategy

- Culture

- Human Resources context

- Prior organizational experience with coaching and development initiatives

- Knowledge and understanding of coaching

If a coach uses these factors to assess the potential of a coaching engagement and decides to move forward with the engagement, the level of success and value to the organization will be increased.

BUSINESS CONTEXT AND STRATEGY

In *Human Resources for the 21st Century* Marc Effron, discussing the potential success of a coaching program, writes, "The purpose of executive coaching (and all leadership practices) should be to align leaders' behaviors with what's required to realize the business strategy."[2] If an organization has a clear, long-term vision, a sound and well-thought-out strategic plan, and achievable goals and objectives to support the strategy, the organization has a solid platform from which to identify leadership competencies and success factors. These competencies should be forward thinking to provide a basis for developmental coaching and for executives to set achievable and meaningful personal goals.

To maximize the effectiveness and value of the coaching engagement, both client and coach need to be aware of the organization's leadership competencies when determining the coaching focus. For example, a 360 feedback assessment might set the stage for what the executive could benefit from working on with the coach. If, say, analytical skills are considered a core competency of the organization, then these may be critical to success for the client. However, if the client's position is not one in which those skills are important, the coach and client may decide not to expend energy in this area, as it has no inherent value in furthering the organization's business objectives.

When I was head of Human Resources at Old Mutual Asset Management, the CEO established a clear strategy for the organization. We were able to identify the necessary competencies to achieve this strategy, which we then embedded into our talent management and executive coaching programs. Thus, our executives knew what they needed to focus on for their own development, as well as to carry out the firm's strategy.

CULTURE OF TRUST

Effective coaching demands a high level of trust. This pertains to the relationship between coach and client, as well as within the organization. Coaching works best in organizations where there is a culture of trust and such values as respect, accountability, and integrity are important. Furthermore, decisions based on these values—along with strategy and goals—rather than on personal views and relationships are important for success. The work that coach and client undertake in partnership should be consistent with the culture and values of the organization. Again, at Old Mutual Asset Management, organizational values were embedded into talent management, creating a culture of trust and respect, and serving as a platform for the firm's executive and employee development initiatives.

Organizations in which trust, respect, et al. are not particularly valued challenge a coach's ability to behave ethically; an organization that uses coaching to obtain information about its employees' performance, for example, puts the coach at risk of violating coach-client confidentiality. This issue should be discussed at the onset to determine whether the coach takes on the coaching engagement.

Another significant factor a coach should pay attention to is whether the organization values its employees and is supportive of learning, change, and growth. The following questions help determine if the culture of the organization is conducive to coaching, and how to best manage the engagement. Does the organization

- Value its employees and their contributions?

- Consider the relationships between employees and their managers and peers important?

- Foster teamwork and collaboration?

- Value performance and emphasize promotion from within?

- Through its vision and strategy, strive to differentiate itself from its competition?

- Strive to create a high-performing environment by investing in its employees through learning and development initiatives?

These are all relevant questions for an external coach to consider when deciding whether to move forward with a coaching engagement. If the organization does not actively support learning and development, nor promote from within, the coach may want to clarify the expectations of the client as to what might be realistic outcomes of the coaching engagement. Or, the coach may decide to work with or influence key stakeholders in the organization about the need for and importance of cultural change (i.e., development of a robust performance management process where feedback is given against goals that are established at the start of a calendar or fiscal year, team coaching to build collaboration and open feedback, etc.).

In my role as a program manager at the leadership development firm Karlin Sloan & Company, I had the opportunity to manage a coaching initiative for a global leader in research and program implementation in the fields of health, social and environmental policy, and international development. The success of the work there was clearly related to the value placed on collaboration and teamwork, how employees' contributions were valued, and a commitment from the top of the organization to the leadership and professional development of all employees. The CEO of the organization was committed to this and practiced what she preached.

HUMAN RESOURCES

In most external coaching engagements, the coach contracts with a key stakeholder (i.e., the CEO or other senior executive) or Human Resources. Where the organizational client is Human Resources, the coach needs to understand not only the position of Human Resources within the organization, but how it is viewed. If Human Resources is not perceived as one of the organization's strategic drivers, the coach may want to develop relationships with other key stakeholders to influence the coaching engagement's success. Where Human Resources is considered to be a critical function, the coach may well benefit from understanding the following:

- Is there a Human Resources strategy aligned with the overall business strategy of the firm?

- Is Human Resources receiving CEO and/or executive support, and are sufficient financial resources provided to strategic Human Resource initiatives?

- Does Human Resources advocate the dissemination and

communication of strategy to employees at all levels, and do Human Resources practices cascade from the strategy?

- Has Human Resources positioned the organization to be an employer of choice—an organization that can attract and retain talent based on its successful business strategy and employee-friendly culture?

- At what level does Human Resources implement best practices in the areas of development and competency models, talent management, feedback and employee communications, and rewards and recognition?

As an external coach develops a systemic perspective of an organization, understanding the role of Human Resources can provide a platform from which to work. For example, if Human Resources supports best practices and a holistic approach to talent management, the work the coach has been contracted to do is an important component of how the organization wants to develop its talent and build its talent pipeline (i.e., filling gaps identified through talent reviews and succession planning exercises). If not, the coach may want to consider advocating best practices to help move the organization forward, and in turn move forward the practice of effective coaching within the organization.

PRIOR ORGANIZATIONAL EXPERIENCE WITH COACHING AND DEVELOPMENT INITIATIVES

Another thing to consider is the organization's prior experience with coaching and learning/development initiatives. In organizations where very visible senior level executives, ideally starting with the CEO, have engaged with coaches, the tone is set from the top. Coaching is aspired to because it is developmental, rather than remedial and a signal an employee is on the way out the door. Not only is support from the top tier important, but their involvement and buy-in in determining who will participate in coaching initiatives is another key factor to look for. In organizations where senior executives and managers play a role in the coaching process, the work between coach and client is more effective.

Beyond experience with external coaching, another relevant factor is whether internal coaching (either by managers or dedicated internal coaches) is valued and institutionalized within the organization. If these factors do not exist, a coach may attempt to engage the top tier of the organization. As Marc Effron recommends in *Human Resources for the 21st Century*, to engage senior leaders "your best approach is to create a coaching business plan . . . and present it to them with a comprehensible way to measure performance. In this plan, be clear about who will be coached and why and how you will be able to measure their success (how we will know someone has changed)."[3]

KNOWLEDGE AND UNDERSTANDING OF COACHING

Another area worth exploring is what coaching practices an organization has in place. A coach evaluating a potential coaching engagement should assess how advanced the organization is in implementing coaching initiatives and how it engages coaches. Questions worth asking:

- Who will participate in the coaching engagement and how are those decisions made?

- How will the coaching engagement be managed by the organization, and who will manage it?

- Is the engagement part of a coaching initiative, and if so, how will the coaching engagement be integrated with the work of other coaches working within the system?

- What types of coaches are currently engaged or have been engaged in the past? What is the experience level of those coaches, and are they credentialed or accredited by a respected coaching organization?

- How does the organization source coaches? Does it rely on independent practitioners, or work with coaching organizations or networks?

- What type of coaching methodology, psychological or behavioral, does the organization subscribe to?

- What assessment instruments are used within the organization or what instruments will be required?

- Is there an established coaching process utilized within the organization? And are there standards in place as to the duration of a coaching engagement?

Answers to these questions provide a coach with a perspective of how the firm looks at coaching best practices, and how to tailor the coaching to the organization's needs. Based on the coach's competencies, the principles the coach follows, and process the coach employs, the coach can determine whether there is a good fit with this organization.

The last area a coach should evaluate is the organization's expectations. This can be critical to a coach's success working within the system, but it is even more important to the client's success. Marshall Goldsmith and Kelly Goldsmith, in their article "Helping People Achieve Their Goals," write, "An important part of this development process includes helping people set—and achieve—meaningful goals for personal change."[4] If the organization places too great a demand on the coach, detracting from the actual coaching work, or has unrealistic expectations of what is achievable, then the engagement may be doomed to failure. As discussed above, trust and confidentiality are key in the coaching process. If the organization's expectations are that the coach will share specific data, and not themes, gathered during the coaching process, then this may be a situation in which the coach may not be able to adhere to an appropriate level of ethical conduct, or focus appropriately on the client's agenda. If these are the expectations of the firm, if the coach is unable to influence these factors, then the coach would be well advised to disengage from the organization.

As I've explored the factors a coach should look for to determine how successful coaching will be within an organization, I've come to understand the challenges a coach faces if he or she is truly going to focus on the client's agenda. Without a deep understanding of the organizational characteristics discussed in this chapter, a coach's work is more challenging and the level of success hampered. The more a coach understands the importance of this, the greater the value he or she can provide the coaching client.

Notes

1. Executive Coaching Forum, *The Executive Coaching Handbook*, 5th ed. (January 2012), 12, accessed October 14, 2013, http://www. theexecutivecoachingforum.com/docs/default-document-library/ echb5thedition2_25.pdf?sfvrsn=0.

2. Marc Effron, "Finding the Missing Link: Connecting Your Business Strategy and Leadership Strategy," in *Human Resources for the 21st Century*, ed. Marc Effron, Robert Gandossy, and Marshall Goldsmith (Hoboken, NJ: John Wiley & Sons, 2003), 215–226.

3. Effron, "Finding the Missing Link."

4. Marshall Goldsmith and Kelly Goldsmith, "Helping People Achieve Their Goals," *Leader to Leader* 39 (Winter 2006): 24. This article is available on the Marshall Goldsmith Library website, accessed October 14, 2013, http://www.marshallgoldsmithlibrary.com/cim/ articles_display.php?aid=282.

Lou Chrostowski is an executive coach and consultant with Karlin Sloan & Company. His past coaching-related positions include head of human resources at Old Mutual Asset Management and chief administrative officer for human resources, Putnam Investments.

6

Adventures in the C Suite: Coaching Executives

John P. Schuster

Over twenty-five years ago, before we used the word coaching, I started working with CEOs in what we called one-on-one settings. During the hundreds of hours I spent sitting across from the CEOs in their offices, I began to get a feel for what the power, limits, and process of coaching entailed. There were no coaching books to read back then, but organizational development professionals, and the accepted literature in the fields of leadership and counseling, informed me about listening and evocative/provocative methods and how they added value to CEOs, their leadership, and their personal and organizational lives.

I had many an adventure in those settings. I still do. And I imagine most coaches do as well, at whatever level we are coaching. Our profession leads to breakthroughs in awareness for our clients, as well as occasional mishaps, laughs, insight. And, I hope, most of all it leads to recovered or discovered layers of their humanity and potential that these leaders need for moving ahead.

We use the term "breakthrough" because of the way ideas and insights sometimes crack through the crust of our surface thinking. But a breakthrough is a process rather than an event. As executives go through their über-busy days, much of their thinking occurs in the moment-to-moment addressing of challenges and opportunities that emerge in meetings, hallway conversations, or the email inbox. Many a client has told me that during their coaching sessions they have a felt sense—they know—that they are thinking at another level of consciousness.

Here is a bit of guidance gathered from what is now well into thousands of hours of coaching one-on-one and in group settings, and from twelve years of teaching coaching skills to approximately a thousand professionals on their way to coaching certification:

- **Go deep** and facilitate the transformational.

- **Play your hunches**, or intuition, with skill.

- **Understand the psychological dimensions** of this human process called coaching.

Go Deep and Facilitate the Transformational

Not all coaching issues need deep coaching, the kind that leads to transformational outcomes. But almost all coaching issues are not very far away from the transformational issues that do require deep coaching. This chart is one way to think of it.

Symptom/Coaching Topic	Blind Spot/ Immediate Cause	Underlying Behavior/ Trait
Time management	Not seeing the role clearly	Being a compulsive doer; unable to handle ambiguity; need more work on values
Conflict with a peer	Not having a broad enough perspective	Having to win and competing, or being overly compliant
Unsupportive boss	Not approaching the boss well	Not fully responsible for self; rejecting authority; never having learned the lessons that come with a poor boss
No time for exercise	Committing to too many goals	Not understanding the reality of limits

Best-sellers have been written about all the issues above. Many pop psychology books about such topics as handling difficult relationships or maximizing time efficiency locate the issues in columns one and two and help people treat the symptoms with rigor.

As coaches, we need to address the symptoms in Column One with our best listening and solution-based coaching. Small and immediate wins build momentum and serve the client. Column Two is where the work of deeper coaching begins and Column Three is where the engagement can be taken to, more often than not, if the coach has the depth to understand that even though a client's most immediate and obvious challenges have been resolved, profound issues may remain. In Column Three we are coaching the client on his or her blind spots and on mental/emotional models, the ones that help clients renew their outlook and refresh their life-long habits.

So as coaches we keep two agendas: the immediate hot stuff, and the deeper slow-burn stuff. By bringing into play Column Three we are working with shadow material—the parts of ourselves of which we are most unaware—where we re-capture what has been lost in the process of adapting to society's norms. It is here that we work for the deepest of transformations.

Billy Joel, pop artist and, unbeknownst to himself, executive coach, wrote in "The River of Dreams":

> *And I've been searching for something*
> *Taken out of my soul*
> *Something I would never lose*
> *Something somebody stole*[1]

Like all poets, Joel conveys an experience that is universal: how those essential pieces of self are lost in the process of living.

Many high-achieving executives have only a dim idea that all humans, including themselves, pay a price for growing up to be "successful." But when these same execs get 360 feedback that they are deeply failing in some aspects of leadership, they often wake up and decide it is time to expand. They don't really know how they are doing and that their blind spots are showing until they get the 360 feedback. Coaching can be the means to recapture what was stolen from their souls.

The word "soul," for a host of reasons, has dropped out of much contemporary dialogue, especially in scientific circles. I do not refer to the "immortal soul" discussed by modern theologians, but the soul discussed by the philosophers of ancient Greece, where "soul" referred to the totality of the human being, the essence residing at the core of the person in the many roles that person plays (executive leadership being one of the big ones we are addressing). We are naïve to think, with our modern ability to measure brain activity during meditative states and our psychological and sociological observations assessing the impact of emotional intelligence, that other, much earlier cultures have not plumbed the depths of human interaction. Let's appreciate the rigors of science and what it brings to coaching, and let us not be afraid to use language that conjures more ambiguous but equally powerful concepts. These ideas can be put to use for ourselves as coaches, and thus for our clients.

The deep Column Three coaching is soul retrieval work. On the surface, the problems of difficult employees and the too-demanding job are obvious. Below the surface, though, is where the real work is.

Coaches have to start where the clients are. We do the superficial work, and then the more challenging work and less superficial work, that everyone can see needs to be done. In the process, we help our clients get more whole and recapture the original possibility of themselves. This is what makes leaders more effective.

PLAY YOUR HUNCHES WITH SKILL

As coaches we are required to learn the science of coaching and practice it as an art. When we discipline ourselves to learn the science, we free ourselves up to play our hunches, use our intuition, and do what is needed in the moment. What will happen can be inside or outside our models and even our understanding. It can be what has to happen in the unique moment of this client in this situation with you, the only coach who could be there at this time. This conversation has never happened in the universe before this and will never happen again.

Let me illustrate with one of my adventures. A few years ago, I was called in to a large nonprofit organization in which the CEO and COO had grown at odds with each other. I was hired by the board to coach the COO. I started with a series of interviews with board members and the vice presidents. The COO was in deep trouble with his CEO, and the interviews revealed he was not performing in a few important areas.

The interviews also revealed that the CEO was notoriously dictatorial, while being quite the visionary. He had been in charge for twenty years.

Having created some rapport with the CEO during the interview about his COO, I held my first joint meeting with the two of them, in which the CEO declared to me and my COO client: "I've told my VP team how unmotivating it is for me that I, for the first time, am not going to receive a bonus from the board because of our poor performance. That just can't happen!"

I was shocked to hear this. The man had hundreds of staff members working for low wages, the recession had kicked in, and the organization was starting to shed staff—many of whom were at this nonprofit to serve the community and the organization's greater mission. And this CEO, known for a bit of ostentation with his wealth, was moaning about his bonus all over the management team.

I realized that this might be my last conversation in this organization, but I had to respond. "Do you realize how unmotivating it is for your staff to hear about your bonus? These people care about the mission of the organization and the community that they serve and to have you talk about your bonus says the wrong things about you as a leader. So I highly recommend that you never say that again and keep your bonus discussion to the board."

The CEO looked at me like he could not take this comment in, so I repeated it, and he got it: "Oh, yeah, I see your point." We returned to the COO discussion, the purpose of our meeting.

Forty-five days later, the CEO told me how great the COO was doing. Five months later the COO was gone, making an elegant exit—there was no longer enough money to pay those two big salaries. And the CEO told me how much he appreciated my leveling with him on the bonus discussion. In this case, I had taken a big risk within a client setting with the client's boss, one of the sponsors of the coaching. I went with my feelings and my hunch, based on years of experience in organizations, about the rift that so often opens between C-suite concerns and the reality of the front line.

My point is a simple one. Use your intuition and play your hunches. I am not sure why I did what I did that day but it worked. I am not sure it was necessary, but I do believe it was good for my client and his boss.

Coaching can go outside the models we have all studied and can be real and value-added in ways that only that moment calls for. Trust yourself to be in the moment and do the right thing—assuming of course you have worked on yourself enough to trust your hunches. Discipline allows you to make hunches.

Finally, forgive yourself when you are wrong with a hunch; if this conversation had blown up on me I still would have had a lesson, wouldn't I? And expect some failures. I have had clients who definitely needed deeper change work as leaders but, try as I might, I could not figure out a way to facilitate that change.

UNDERSTAND THE PSYCHOLOGICAL DIMENSIONS OF COACHING

Over the years coaching has stayed away from therapy, for good reason. But that does not mean coaching can stay away from psychology. Leadership is all about psychology and human needs and inclinations, and coaching can be no different. *Coach and Couch: The Psychology of Making Better Leaders*, by Manfred Kets de Vries et al., is a worthwhile read on this topic. He writes:

> Our unconscious plays a tremendous role in determining our actions, thoughts; fantasies, hopes and fears... Moreover, the unconscious can hold executives as prisoners of their own past...
>
> The clinical paradigm can be described metaphorically as a way of exploring a person's "inner theater." Behind the curtain, we all have a rich tragi-comedy playing out on our inner stage, with key actors representing the people we have loved, hated, feared, and admired. Early experiences are re-enacted over and over again. . . . Every executive and every employee brings their inner theater, with all its dramas and comedies, to the workplace. Dysfunctional behavior arises when we try to keep the curtain closed...[2]

As an analyst who coaches executives, Kets de Vries faces all the issues that most executive coaches face: workaholic patterns, narcissism, tough decisions, strategies that are in question. As a champion of "therapeutically informed" coaching, he argues that coaches without a knowledge of the unconscious are selling the work and their clients short.

I could not agree more. My quest to get informed psychologically led me to Jungian psychology and the degree programs in humanistic and Jungian psychology at Saybrook University. My first real mentor in coaching, Frederic Hudson of the Hudson Institute, saw the forty-year-old version of me and advised me "to get more psychological." I only dimly understood what he was driving at as he observed my too-shallow understanding of the workings of the psyche. More than twenty years later, I get it, and I see many an aspiring coach who is seduced by the presenting problem (Column One, remember) and misses the inner theater where the action is.

The language of leadership development lends itself to psychological theories. Much leadership work uses narrative techniques, which allow and encourage work on memories, even those outside the client's awareness. Leadership work reviews critical incidents—mentors, bad bosses, and, most importantly, assignments, failed and successful alike—which all carry both positive and negative emotional charges and mental models from the past into the leader's present style.

The leadership field also uses somatic approaches, such as breathing and presence, to get past the simple thoughts of shallow consciousness into deeper layers of awareness. It uses metaphor (think of Ronald Heifetz's idea of "getting on the balcony"), allowing entry into imagery and fantasy. And it explores espoused values versus lived values, so the neurotic splits between a will that intends something (espoused values) and the actual behavior (lived values) are ready material for coaches to explore. Psychological hangups are often called, in corporate-speak, blind spots or career derailers, and such language makes the "inner theater" of the leader available for the coach.

So what does "understand psychology" mean for us in the mainstream of coaching? Go back to school to study? Work with a therapist? Perhaps, but that is not what I am really urging us to do. I offer three suggestions:

- **Constantly work on your own awareness.** Leave no stone unturned in examining every bit of anxiety, stressful communication, or repetitive behavior—including doing too much work—that you experience. Get to its root. Journal about it. Work with a deep coach, a psychologically sophisticated coach, as a supervisor to work on Self.

- **Don't be fooled as a coach that what you are hearing the client present as the challenge or opportunity is the real challenge.** What it's about is never what it is about. That is how my Jungian teacher James Hollis puts it. So go back to the first part of this essay on going deep. Column Three is the psychological domain.

- **What you see is a compensation for what you don't see.** This is another Hollis truth. This means to me, among other things, that our competent leader clients, looking and sounding very much on the outside like they have it together, have an inner theater that is much different from what we all see. The narcissist is insecure, the control freak manager has an empowering side, the hard-core politically inclined leader has an authentic vulnerability.

Have some great adventures, coaches. The privilege of coaching comes entwined with a large amount of responsibility to work on yourself and see deeply into the human being who has entrusted you with a developmental conversation. Be responsible and become worthy of your work and of your client. Develop yourself continually.[3]

NOTES

1. This is the title song to the album *The River of Dreams*, released August 10, 1993. The Billy Joel website, accessed October 25, 2013, http://www.billyjoel.com/music/river-dreams/river-dreams.

2. Manfred F. R. Kets de Vries and Konstantin Korotov, "The Clinical Paradigm: A Primer For Personal Change," in *Coach and Couch: The Psychology of Making Better Leaders*, Manfred F. R. Kets de Vries, Konstantin Korotov, and Elizabeth Florent-Treacy, INSEAD Business Press Series (Basingstoke, UK: Palgrave Macmillan, 2007), 3–5.

3. A general framework for the ideas of this article can be found in my book *The Power of Your Past: The Art of Recalling, Reclaiming and Recasting* (San Francisco: Berrett-Koehler, 2011).

John Schuster is a practicing executive coach who is also a faculty member at both the Hudson Institute of Coaching (Santa Barbara) and the Columbia Coaching Certification Program, Columbia University. His most recent books are *The Power of Your Past: The Art of Recalling, Reclaiming and Recasting* (2011) and *Answering Your Call: A Guide to Living Your Deepest Purpose* (2003), both published by Berrett-Koehler (San Francisco).

7

Contracting for the Coaching Engagement: Key Considerations in an Organizational Setting

By Denise Verolini, Patricia M. Armstrong, Nancy Amick, Stephanie Duignan and Lorilee Mills

This chapter is devoted to the special considerations involved in establishing clear goals and boundaries for coaching engagements that take place within an organizational setting. When coaching is provided by or through a client's employer, stakeholders beyond the coach and client dyad should be actively engaged in both the contracting and coaching process. In this chapter we define contracting as an essential pre-coaching process, we recommend a series of questions designed to identify and integrate the goals and expectations of all the stakeholders, and we describe the design of a comprehensive coaching agreement that will serve as a common reference point for all those involved with the coaching process. We also highlight those circumstances under which it may be preferable to defer a coaching engagement.

CONTRACTING: A PRE-COACHING PROCESS

Contracting is a discovery process that typically takes place prior to the beginning of any coaching engagement. This process can be defined as a conversation among a proposed coach, client and one or more stakeholders that answers the questions, Why coaching? Why now? Who will be involved? How will confidentiality be maintained? If the coaching is successful, what will it address or solve? Contracting is a particularly important process when the engagement occurs within an organizational setting. Under these circumstances, coaches have multiple clients to consider during any one coaching engagement. Therefore, who is included in the engagement and the parameters of confidentiality are critical discussion points during the pre-coaching process.

The contracting or needs assessment process helps determine whether coaching is the right solution for the presenting issue. If the decision is made to proceed, this assessment will provide a strong foundation that will serve the client, coach and sponsor(s) throughout the course of the engagement. A thorough needs assessment will uncover information regarding goals, roles and the coaching process as key stakeholders discuss desired outcomes, understand how information will be shared, and express their level of support for the engagement. This needs assessment process naturally leads to a coaching agreement, or the decision that coaching is not the right solution at this time.

If coaching is the agreed-upon action, a coaching agreement provides a directional map of where the coaching is headed, allows for progress to be measured, and creates stakeholder accountability. It is recommended that the contracting discussions conclude with the preparation of a written, signed agreement that succinctly captures the answers to seven key needs assessment questions described below. The structure of this agreement will support the entire coaching engagement. While it is possible to amend some aspects of the agreement as the engagement proceeds, it is important to retain the original intent and alignment because, without this structure, the engagement can devolve into a loosely defined series of meetings that meander into and out of organizational relevance – an outcome that no one intends, but that too often occurs when structure is absent.

If the contracting process uncovers a substantive difference of stakeholder opinion regarding coaching goals, or surfaces a lack of commitment from any stakeholder, the engagement should be postponed or cancelled. It is far more advantageous to surface key issues before the coaching begins rather than once the engagement is underway, as differing agendas may limit the desired outcomes from the coaching engagement. It is useful to all stakeholders to clarify why moving forward with the engagement is inadvisable. On some occasions, a delay in the onset of coaching gives stakeholders an opportunity to get clear and aligned around what needs to change or be developed with an executive.

COACHING NEEDS ASSESSMENT

The following seven questions address the readiness of the key stakeholders to begin the coaching process. For each question, we've described a recommended inquiry process, identified a corresponding "test" to be passed in order to proceed, and offered some cautionary notes.

1. Why do the executive and his/her manager need or want coaching now?

Executive coaching that achieves its intended impact begins with an open dialogue and agreement about the "why." Why coaching? Why now? What occurred that made someone consider coaching? What outcomes do stakeholders expect coaching to produce? Ideally, the potential client, manager, and, when applicable, the human resources professional have discussed these questions in some detail and agreed that coaching is the best option for taking action. Even when these discussions have taken place individually, it is important to repeat the agreements with everyone present.

This first question, when given proper attention, also provides the coach a lens through which to view the potential client and manager including the quality of their communication. If the coach finds common ground in the objectives of both the client and manager, there is not only a green light to proceed to the second inquiry, but the coach can be cautiously optimistic that the relationship between the manager and the client is, at a minimum, strong enough to pass the first test: the degree of alignment about the purpose of coaching.

However, in situations where a coach is hired with the hope of addressing a challenge associated with the executive, it is common to discover that the problematic issue, or the degree of concern about the issue, has not been communicated to the client. In these instances, the manager will often tell the human resources professional and/or coach that he or she has *attempted* to communicate the concern to the client but somehow the message has not been received: e.g. *"I've tried to tell this executive many times ... but he has not heard me. Maybe a coach can give it a try."* Or, *"I have not been able to find the best way to communicate to this executive and I need the coach to do it on my behalf."* If the contracting process surfaces concerns regarding this first of seven questions, it may be useful to pause before proceeding with the engagement. Should the coach be overly willing to begin, he or she could unwittingly be agreeing to be the messenger for the manager – a role ill-fated for any coach.

2. Who are the key stakeholders and what are the expectations for each of them?

Each coaching engagement within an organizational setting typically involves a minimum of four professionals, and often more if the client manages others or is a member of a team. Typically the coach, the coaching client, the client's manager and human resources professional are the key players in the coaching engagement, all with slightly different roles. When all parties to the coaching engagement demonstrate a commitment to the client's success, the coach has secured a second green light in the contracting phase. The test to be passed here is one of willingness to invest in the client. The coach must describe the degree of involvement needed during and after the engagement. For example, stakeholders are often asked to observe the client and provide feedback to him or her throughout the engagement, and are periodically asked to participate in meetings with the client and coach to discuss progress made on the coaching objectives. All parties must agree to undertake these important activities.

3.   How will success, or lack of success, be defined and measured?

Contracting involves naming specific indicators of coaching success. What are the stakeholders expecting to occur as a result of the coaching? These indicators are often a combination of business results, executive behaviors, or other observable results. Specificity is critical so that as the engagement unfolds, stakeholders are able to assess the degree of progress toward the desired result. With well-defined goals, desired changes should be evident to the stakeholders long before the engagement has concluded, and ideally in time to modify the coaching activities should there be a lack of progress.

A tone of optimism is common during the initial phases of coaching. This is good to see because it demonstrates hope for the needed change, but it is advisable for the coach to caution the client and stakeholders about unguarded optimism. The possibility of negative as well as positive outcomes should be acknowledged, and more importantly, must be intentionally discussed during the contracting phase, e.g. *"What will happen if the agreed-upon results are not achieved through coaching?"*

Executives often avoid discussing the possibility of failure. It is simply not a comfortable conversation, especially when a coach has been hired to create positive change. Yet, speaking openly about failure as a possibility, discussing what failure would look like, and then talking about the impact, should it occur, is an essential aspect of contracting.

This discussion allows stakeholders to think about the importance of the identified coaching goals. Even during this pre-coaching contracting process, the coach can frame the risk and reward conversation in ways that begin to change habits of thinking and increases stakeholders' investment in the client and the organization. The test to be passed here is whether the stakeholders are clear and aligned about what they want to have happen as a result of the coaching, as well as what may happen if the coaching does not achieve the results everyone has agreed are important to the client and the business.

4. What business needs will be satisfied by a successful coaching engagement?

In every kind of coaching, success is defined by the degree to which the coaching achieves predetermined goals. Executive coaching, however, is distinguished by the expectation that an engagement will create an impact for the organization, as well as for the individual client, before it can be deemed successful. This critically important link between coaching success and business outcomes is one of the hallmarks of the field and, as such, must be supported by goals that include both the executive and the organization. The test to be passed here is whether the coaching engagement can create benefit for the organization as well as the individual.

5. How will confidentiality be preserved?

The foundation of effective coaching is the trust that develops between coach and client, and in an organizational setting, between the coach and other stakeholders as well. Trust is fostered when the client experiences freedom to disclose challenges or reactions without concern that the coach may share this information with the client's manager or other members of the organization. Simultaneously, the coach must have the freedom, throughout the engagement, to speak with stakeholders about the client's progress toward the coaching goals. If the coach can navigate this tricky terrain, all stakeholders benefit and the engagement will have a strong foundation. The coach supports the formation of a trusting relationship by reaching clarity about confidentiality before the engagement begins, clearly addressing how coaching goals and progress will be discussed with others, and reaching agreement on specific communication practices that will be non-negotiable.

Three key aspects of confidentiality should be covered in the contracting phase. All three describe who discusses what, with whom, and under which circumstances. Together these form what can be thought of as the mutually understood and agreed upon boundaries that will be adhered to during the coaching engagement.

i. **Coach and client "protected space."** The client is encouraged to use the coach as a sounding board, and is entitled to have a safe haven where information he or she reveals is not disclosed to anyone else. Clarifying any exceptions to this agreement is essential, and may include legal and ethical considerations that can arise.

ii. **Organization as client.** When the organization provides executive coaching, the organization is the coach's primary client, and the coach is thus expected to report how the client and the coaching are progressing in relationship to the mutually agreed upon coaching goals.

iii. **No messengers.** The coach should clearly establish that he or she will not serve as a messenger among stakeholders, and encourage all stakeholders to adhere to this guideline with one another. The coach can, however, assist all stakeholders in determining how best to communicate directly and more effectively with one another.

In general, it is advisable that with all stakeholders other than the client, the coach stay primarily in the role of receiver, versus the deliverer of information by asking questions and gathering information throughout the engagement. This is a safe and useful position to take that supports clear boundaries between coach and client, and coach and stakeholders. The test to be passed here is of utmost importance to the coach's credibility and effectiveness: Can the coach and all stakeholders agree to maintain the boundaries of communication? If confidentiality is compromised, the engagement is placed in serious jeopardy.

5. What activities will occur during the beginning, middle and end of the engagement?

Although much of what occurs within the engagement is determined by the client and the nature of the issues and goals, coaching practitioners have established a basic structure that helps create a sense of flow during the coaching engagement including activities such as gathering 360 feedback about the client, coach observation and meetings with key stakeholders.

A willingness to give and receive feedback is an important part of any coaching engagement. The test here is threefold:

i. **Is the client willing to receive feedback through multiple means such as 360 feedback and observation by others?**

ii. **Are stakeholders willing to share their candid feedback and observations with the client?**

iii. **Can the coach help the client navigate through the feedback, particularly if any part of it is surprising to them or is something they perceive as unjustified? If the client has any retaliatory inclinations as a result of the feedback, the coach must discover this and take an active role in understanding the reaction and helping the client through the potential outcomes of responding in a negative or retaliatory manner.**

This realistic preview of the extent to which the coaching engagement will involve ongoing collection and review of stakeholder feedback throughout the duration of the engagement is a critical aspect of contracting in an organizational setting. The preview sets the expectation that the ability to integrate and take positive action based on constructive feedback is both an expectation and an integral part of the coaching process.

7. How long will the engagement last and how much will it cost?

Depending on the coaching goals and sense of urgency, an approximate time frame should be agreed on at the beginning of the engagement. A range of six to eighteen months is typical in an organizational setting. Fees should be negotiated during the contracting phase so that all stakeholders are clear about the price of the engagement. There should also be an explicit discussion regarding whether coaching will be paid for by the client or the client's manager. When a client's manager pays for the cost of coaching, it sends the message that coaching is an investment in the client, and that the engagement is fully supported by the manager.

This discussion of time frame and cost are a test of the manager's commitment to the coaching process, and is an important discussion not just for the coach, but for the other stakeholders who need to understand what they and their organization are getting, and at what cost. This investment of time and fees helps everyone to have skin in the game.

COMPLETING THE WRITTEN COACHING AGREEMENT

The written coaching agreement typically contains the following:

- **Coaching objectives**
- **Parameters of confidentiality**
- **Duration and cost of coaching**
- **Responsible party for assuming the cost of coaching**
- **Frequency of meetings with the client and key stakeholders**

A valuable practice is to review the coaching agreement within the first few weeks of the coaching engagement during a meeting with the client, the client's manager, the coach and when applicable, the client's human resources manager.[1] By reviewing the coaching agreement and coaching objectives together in the early weeks of the coaching engagement, the goal is to create early alignment among all parties and a solid foundation and structure for the coaching engagement.

A sample coaching agreement is provided below to illustrate the way in which the contracting process can be summarized in a written agreement.

Executive Transition Coaching Agreement
[Sample Coaching Agreement for a new-in-role leader offered
coaching to support success in this new leadership role.]

Executive Coaching Client: John Smith

Executive Coach:

Sponsor/Manager: HR Manager:

Start Date: Anticipated End Date:

Cost: Account to Charge:

JOHN'S EXECUTIVE COACHING OBJECTIVES

- Create and communicate a vision statement and strategy to help the team focus on activities that will drive business results; business goals include an increase of x% in the profit plan

- Assess the individual capabilities of team members in key positions to determine their strengths and challenges; create targeted coaching and/or development plans for each

- Close the gap between self-perception and perceptions of others: build credibility as a trusted leader, increase awareness of impact on others and increase followership one relationship at a time

EXECUTIVE COACHING PROCESS

- John and Coach will meet weekly by phone or in-person for the first half of the coaching engagement; 2-3x per month for the second half

- Coach will meet with John in-person as needed

- Coach will observe John in different settings to share observations of strengths and areas for ongoing development to support a successful transition

- John's Manager, HR Partner, John and Coach will meet at the onset of executive coaching to ensure alignment of expectations and support; at least once during the executive coaching engagement to discuss progress and specific ways each can continue to support John; and at the end of executive coaching to review progress and determine next steps for continued success

- If needed, Coach will interview John's direct report team and key partners for the purpose of obtaining feedback regarding the current state of John's team and business and what type of leadership is needed. Feedback will be used to inform the coaching objectives

- At the end of the executive coaching engagement, 360 feedback will be considered and/or Coach will integrate any previous 360 feedback into the coaching work

CONFIDENTIALITY

- Coach will not disclose specific content of executive coaching meetings except under the following circumstances:

  — Coach will provide John's Manager and HR Partner with an assessment of John's progress toward the executive coaching objectives including any trends or themes noticed during the executive coaching engagement

  — Coach will also offer suggestions to John's Manager and HR Partner about how they can best coach and support John in order to help him be most effective in his role

Note:

*Human resources roles vary across organizations. When a business partner model of human resources is employed, this partner may be able to assist with the integration of relevant feedback across stakeholders and the alignment of the coaching process with business needs.

Patricia M. Armstrong is the managing director of family dynamics at Abbot Downing, a Wells Fargo business serving the needs of ultra-high-net-worth families and individuals, endowments, and foundations.

Prior to her current role Pat was the head of human resources for the wealth management business of Wells Fargo. Pat holds a doctorate in counseling psychology from Southern Illinois University.

Stephanie Duignan is a senior vice president and manager of talent, diversity and organizational development at Wells Fargo in Wealth, Brokerage and Retirement; she manages the overall strategy for executive and leadership development initiatives, including succession planning, early talent planning, diversity and inclusion, organizational development, and executive coaching. Stephanie holds a master's degree in organizational psychology from the California School of Professional Psychology.

Denise P. Verolini is a senior vice president and the director of team member experience at Wells Fargo Private Bank. She partners with and provides support to a diverse group of cross-functional teams. Denise earned her doctorate in clinical psychology from the California School of Professional Psychology.

Nancy J. Amick is an organizational development consultant and executive coach at Wells Fargo in Wealth, Brokerage and Retirement. She holds a doctorate in clinical psychology from the California School of Professional Psychology.

Lorilee Mills is an organizational development consultant and executive coach at Wells Fargo in Wealth, Brokerage and Retirement, developing customized strategies for leaders and teams. Lorilee holds a bachelors degree in psychology from Iowa State University.

8

Using Assessments for Executive and Organizational Coaching

Kathryn R. Wankel

Feedback is a gift. Being in a role to provide feedback and the related coaching is a privilege not to be treated lightly—but to be honored and respected. Providing 360 feedback and coaching for a major part of my career has been just that—a gift and a privilege and this chapter allows me to share some lessons and best practices around those experiences.

Graduating from Columbia Business School's Executive Coaching Certification Program (CCCP) and earning their Organizational Psychology Masters, combined with 25 years of experience growing leadership pipelines and transitioning leaders in, up, and around two major New York City financial institutions, has informed my work as a practitioner in the use of various forms of assessments to coach executives, transition leaders, build teams, manage change, and assess organizational capabilities.

Before the explosion of this relatively new profession of "Executive and Organizational Coaching", as Human Resource, Talent or "Personnel" professionals, we often found ourselves in various forms of coaching and counseling of employees. Whether it be as a side bar conversation that emerged from a leadership development program; a career counseling discussion around a move; a discussion around performance management; or an employee relations challenge.... coaching happened. Organizational leaders continue to be the real front-line cadre of coaches, while "Talent and Learning Management" professionals also coach as they manage the human capital and related talent development agenda. Those are roles I grew up in as a pioneer internal coach, feedback provider, and go-to people developer.

Spending a lifetime of holding the space for clients, patients, participants, learners, leaders, and/or career searchers as they dreamt, worked- through, discovered, explored, vented, co-created or moved on in their careers (and lives) has given me joy. Often, as part of those varied transitions and conversations some form of "assessment" added value. Assessments add insight that foster learning and related action or movement. They come in many shapes and sizes. This chapter will let us try some on.

In executive coaching, whether it is with an individual or a group, the use of assessment instruments, surveys, and various coaching tools are informed by the expressed goals of the engagement, the organizational context, availability of existing data, the integrity of assessment instruments, and the requisite skills of the coaching professional.

Assessments have been used for years by psychologists and other behavioral professionals. An assessment can be broadly defined as information gathering that serves to evaluate a person against particular standards or guidelines. For example, to try to understand how a person is likely to act or react, or to help the assessed individual be more interpersonally effective. In an organizational setting, assessments are generally used to understand the connection between personality and performance.

An assessment tool is a test or other "instrument" used to accomplish the assessment; when used as part of the coaching process, assessments are often referred to as coaching tools. There are hundreds of assessment tools on the market, measuring everything from people-management skills to test-taking effort—this last one recently advertised as using "dot counting" to detect lack of effort.

The coach can be viewed as an "instrument", as he or she engages in the conscious use-of-self to forward the coaching agenda. Coaches and consultants have a responsibility to choose the best vehicle to help the client gain insight, perspective, self-awareness or behavior change, and not a practice or assessment merely because it is familiar. The big question is, are you using the tool for the good of the client?

Choosing Assessments for Large Scale Organizational Coaching

So, what are the criteria for selecting an information-gathering assessment, practice or process? In large scale and organizational coaching efforts tied to leadership development or change management efforts, leaders/learners, and related talent development sponsors should connect with the coaching practitioners and any related organization development or design consultants (where appropriate) early in the engagement process to ensure all stakeholders agree with the approach and related information-gathering tools and practices to be used. This will ensure alignment with the organization's business needs, culture, values, and goals.

Those decisions become more critical the wider the coaching, change, or development effort is spread through the organization. The related language, competencies, and lens associated with the assessment tools used have larger implications. We get what we measure. Accordingly, in development efforts we want to make sure we measure the right behaviors, dimensions, competencies, and skills.

For example: For many years a financial institution used a certain personality survey instrument in combination with a competency model that provided feedback on a set of sixty-seven leadership behaviors. Before cascading it down into the organization and related performance management system, they did their homework to ensure they measured what mattered and what, if anything, could derail a leader. Because most of the organization's leaders now had experience with those tools and the language associated with them, it became part of the culture to know one's "type" and part of the way feedback was provided in performance management.

Later on, a new consultant attempted to cascade a different tool into courses that looked at career strengths. That tool came with its own set of language and behaviors, with definitions for terms that were foreign to what had become a part of the way people spoke about behaviors, skills, and competencies. Accordingly, different parts of the organization were measuring different skills and behaviors and had different terms for similar things. The result was confusion rather than clarity about what leadership skills should look like, and what mattered for success.

To further complicate the matter, the next consulting firm that began to make its way into the mix introduced yet another tool of its preference. The result was even more confusion. This is not to say always stick with one tool or assessment, but to be aware of the implications when using assessment for large-scale change or development efforts and the potential impact on performance management and any related leadership behaviors.

CHOOSING AN ASSESSMENT FOR EXECUTIVE COACHING

We know that you get what you measure. But there are hundreds of assessments and coaching tools to choose from. Which ones for which goals?

Coaching sets out to foster self-awareness, to provide an arena in which to examine behaviors, intentions, and impact, and to investigate change options that will affect the client's ability to perform in alignment with organizational needs. Accordingly, there exists many varieties of assessments to offer insights and perspectives on a variety of behaviors, dimensions, styles, characteristics, competencies, skills, motivations, values, and tendencies.

There are a number of questions to consider in selecting the right assessment(s) for the situation. These questions center around the overarching coaching goal, the information needed to shape the coaching process, the integrity of the instrument, and the skill of the coach in using it.

SELECTING ASSESSMENTS: QUESTIONS TO CONSIDER

QUESTIONS TO CONSIDER WHEN SELECTING ASSESSMENTS
❖ What is the coaching goal?
❖ What is the budget and timeframe for information gathering?
❖ What are the organization's desired leadership competencies and performance standards?
❖ What language, framework, and leadership/change models does the organization support/use/need?
❖ What assessment tool, method, or process has the client used before?
❖ Which tool or process am I best trained to administer, use, debrief?
❖ What exactly does the assessment measure?
❖ What are the related credibility, research, process, norm base, and/or theory the tool is based from?
❖ Is the instrument valid, reliable, bias free and discrimination free?

❖ How do I plan to use the results to inform the coaching agenda?
❖ What tools or processes am I not considering that I should?
❖ Do I really need to use an instrument or is the data available?
❖ What should I consider that I have not about assessment tool/process?
❖ Who will see the data and for what purpose?
❖ How will confidentiality be maintained?

ASSEESSMENT DATA SOURCES

The formal assessment tool or survey instrument is not, of course, the only source of information the coach will use during the engagement. The client him- or herself has data and personal goals for the process. The client's direct manager can provide observations and expectations. The Talent Management sponsor has organizational data, performance standards, expectations, and guidelines about what behaviors are rewarded or will not be tolerated. Shadowing the client, where the coach spends time observing him or her interact within their organizational system, their team, and observe the interpersonal and relational dynamics in which they lead, is another powerful source of information.

The client's individual development plan and related goals supply data. There may be internal performance evaluations, past 360 feedback or multi-rater feedback reports, turnover numbers, and climate survey results to review. The main coaching agenda itself provides insight to help co-create a coaching plan and related action items that may inform the use of a certain type or assessment modality.

As the coaching engagement progresses, the coach dances through the investigative discovery process with the client, and makes his or her own observations of behaviors and interactions. Feedback and observations emerge. As the coaching development plan unfolds, changing and often being re-negotiated as new information presents itself, more assessment data arises. The three-way coaching plan discussion meeting of coach, client, and client manager is another potential information gathering vehicle for assessment purposes.

Given the personal nature of the coaching process and the coach's individual style, experience, approach, and the number of methods and tools available, it is important to remember there is no single valid approach to any given situation. Two different coaches might successfully apply different methods and tools to the same situation. When serving as an internal coaching professional, my preferences emerged over years of practice using mainly qualitative interviews with stakeholders as assessment in combination with self-assessment instruments to help the client digest feedback and to better understand his or her styles and preferences. Together, we made decisions about whom to interview and the potential and most powerful 360 feedback questions to ask stakeholders to move the coaching agenda forward. Given the client's developmental framework and past experience with training, feedback practices, or tools, we decided the best way to proceed and what additional information was needed.

At times, the "professor-like" coach may emerge for a moment to suggest a form of a custom, co-created "homework assignment" to gather assessment data of a sort that may be as simple as to reflect on a specific set of behaviors, feelings, or goals that could be considered as serving as a form of self-assessment to meet current needs.

Gathering 360 feedback data through stakeholder one-on-one interviews combined with a "debrief" of those interviews and the Myers-Briggs Type Indicator (MBTI Step One or Two) was often my approach of choice. The MBTI based on Carl Jung's theory of personality type looks at where one gets their energy from (introversion/extroversion); how they gather data (sensing or intuiting) , where they go to when making decisions (head or heart); and how they manage their world (scheduled or emergent). Understanding those insights and preferences allowed us to clarify and inform the coaching plan, goals, and related action items. There, we often began to form the related self-awareness pathway around leadership styles and impact.

Many coaching efforts fall into one of several areas:

- Transitioning into a new or different leadership role

- Strengthening some self-management aspect

- Enhancing interpersonal effectiveness and the related impact, and/or

- Developing leadership behaviors or competencies.

Accordingly, the qualitative 360s and a look at style preferences, for me, provided a solid foundation for this human partnership.

If conflict concerns emerge, the Thomas-Kilmann Conflict (TKI) self-assessment can shed light on those challenges and the related conflict styles. A client who wants to look at career challenges can consider several career assessment instruments in addition to the MBTI such as the Gallup's Strengths Finder tool, the Strong-Campbell Interest Inventory, or the Self-Directed Search (SDS) tool.

When emotional intelligence (EI or EQ) is a learning goal, a number of assessments consider EI skills and help to assess those dynamics. When the coaching engagement could benefit from a full look at values, job fit, motivations, styles under pressure, or critical thinking—the Hogan suite of tools referred to as the HPI, HDS, MVPI (and the HBRI for critical thinking) each measure such items. To measure similar areas, the Birkman Method provides different lenses. The Wagner Enneagram Personality Styles tool also takes a comprehensive view of many preferences and factors that impact effectiveness.

Table I within this chapter provides more detail on these widely-used assessments and methods, whom to contact to learn more about the specifics of what they measure, and any certifications or training required for use.

The Neethling Brain Instrument (NBI) is but one of several tools assessing thinking styles. Acumen Leadership Workstyles measures constructive styles and related challenges with tasks and people.

If a client has the results of any relevant assessments he or she has already taken, it might help to ask to see those. Of course, the coach and client would work together to determine any relevance from past assessments to the current state, coaching goals, and current agenda. How long ago was that data gathered? Who were the respondents or stakeholders? Who administered it for what goal? What insights, actions, and/or behavior change took place from the past assessment experience? How was it used and was it debriefed in a productive manner?

TABLE I WIDELY-USED COACHING ASSESSMENT TOOLS AND METHODS

ASSESSMENT TOOL OR PROCESS	POTENTIAL COACHING USE	CONTACT TO LEARN MORE
PERSONALITY		
Myers –Briggs Type Indicator (MBTI) Step One	Psychometric personality survey designed to measure preferences of four dichotomies	CPP Inc. Publisher
Myers –Briggs Type Indicator (MBTI) Step Two	Extended version of MBTI for additional depth & clarification within original four pairs to clarify best fit type	CPP Inc. Publisher
The Disc Assessment	Explores four domains of dominance, influence, steadiness, & compliance. Similar to MBTI	Disc Distributors
Behaviors/ Motivation/Needs		
The Birkman Method	Explores five perspectives of productive behaviors, stress behaviors, underlying needs, motivations & organizational orientation	Birkman International
Hogan Personality Inventory (HPI) (HDS), & (MVPI)	To look at personality; risks and potential derailers; and motivation (core values, goals, interests)	Performance Programs, Inc and Hogan Assessments
Wagner Enneagram Personality Styles (WEPSS)	To identify interpersonal dynamics, work preferences, coping styles, values, and learning styles with nine type's adaptive and maladaptive characteristics noted.	by Jerome P. Wagner, Ph. D.
Work style		

The Acumen Leadership Workstyles	Measuring personal attitudes, thinking, and work style behaviors related to effective leadership	Human Synergistics
Learning/Thinking		
Choices	Assessment of learning agility to learn from experience	Lominger/Korn Ferry International
Neethling Brain Instruments (NBI)	Whole brain thinking profile for insight into thinking preferences on a quadrant noting a rational, practical, relational, and/or experimental profile	Whole Brain Thinking Pty Ltd
Hogan Business Reasoning Inventory (HBRI)	Critical thinking	Hogan Assessments
Conflict Style		
Thomas-Kilmann Conflict Mode Instrument (TKI)	Conflict handling styles and impact	CPP Inc. Publisher
Behaviors/ Competencies		
Voices	Extensive 360 assessment tool based on 67 leadership competencies with respondent comments	Lominger/Korn Ferry International
Qualitative Interviewing With Stakeholders	To get real data from respondents through powerful questions	Coaching Certifications And Skill At Interviewing With Objectivity
Custom 360, Upward, Or Multi-Rater Tools	Organization specific competency focused evaluation process- quantitative look at behaviors with some comments or without	Customize or create own instruments with trained professionals or vendors
Emotional Intelligence		

Emotional And Social Competency Inventory (ESCI)	A 360 to measure emotional and social intelligence	Hay Group, Daniel Goleman, Richard Boyatzis
Career		
Gallup's Strengths Finder	To better understand inherent or natural strengths	Gallup
Strong Campbell Interest Inventory	To look at career interests	CPP Inc. Publishers
Self-Directed Search (SDS)	Career exploration	Based on John L. Holland's theory of careers

CULTURE AND DIVERSITY ASSESSMENTS

Over the years, more organizations have recognized the importance of both diversity and global cultural competence. Accordingly, more assessment instruments have been designed to align corporate cultures. The Lominger/Korn Ferry "Strategic Effectiveness Architect" (eSEA) helps to align organizational capabilities and people practices with strategy and customer value.

To assess individuals on related diversity and cultural awareness competencies, there are several other assessments on the market. The Intercultural Development Inventory (IDI) is a 50 –item, cross cultural measure of intercultural competence. The Culture in the Workplace (CWQ) by Dr. Geert Hofstede, a Dutch Social Scientist, helps understand one's own culture and the impact of culture on the actions of others-as well as on global business interactions. The Cultural Navigator assessment helps to understand cultural preferences and to build the related self-awareness. It can identify potential cultural challenges and strategies to address them. It also helps to collaborate with peers and clients in other cultures.

On the diversity assessment front are two of many instruments: the "ATDS" and the "DAP". The Attitudes Towards Diversity Scale (ATDS) is a ten- item assessment representing three domains around an individual's attitudes toward diversity with regard to coworkers, supervisors, and in hiring and promotion decisions. The Diversity Awareness Profile (DAP) allows one to do an honest assessment of their attitudes and behaviors towards others through a six-paged, self-assessment on an "awareness spectrum" created by Karen M. Stinson. Most recently assessments of cultural and diversity is an expanding area. Table II below provides basic information about some of the widely used assessment tools in this area.

Table II Assessments of Culture and Diversity

Assessment	Potential Use	Contact Information
"Strategic Effectiveness Architect"(eSEA)	Organization Alignment	Korn Ferry/Lominger
Intercultural Development Inventory (IDI)	Cultural Competence	M. R. Hammer & M.J. Bennett
Culture in the Workplace (CWQ)	Cultural Competence	Itap international
Cultural Navigator	Cultural Preferences	Cultural Navigator. com
Attitudes Towards Diversity Scale (ATDS)	Diversity Attitudes	Epm.sagepub.com, Central Michigan University
Diversity Awareness Profile (DAP)	Diversity Attitudes	Pfeiffer.com, Second Edition

Objectivity is essential to the effective use of assessments and other coaching tools. Other than a few web-based virtual coaches and psychologists services (via avatars), the coach is usually a human being, complete with preferences, styles, competencies, and values. Obviously, the coach should be self-aware and unbiased when debriefing instruments and providing feedback.

For example, a coach with a strong preference for a certain thinking style or set of operating principles or values might unknowingly express his or her preferred style as the best practice, when in fact there is no one best way to proceed, view a situation, or achieve a goal.

If a coach takes an instrument and learns he or she is low on competition, power, and approval, it will be important to be aware of those preferences when working with a client who is challenged with influence and taking charge. The coach will need to recognize that people preferring a collaborative style might not consider exploring a new pathway or trying on certain new behaviors that might be needed in a competitive environment where political savvy is imperative.

WHAT DO ASSESSMENTS TRY TO MEASURE?

Assessments fall into a variety of buckets: cognitive, personality, and emotional intelligence (EI or EQ). Overall, there is an attempt to understand some inherent traits; how someone solves problems or accomplishes tasks; and/or some social elements around interaction with others. Assessments are used for a variety of initiatives such as team building, career coaching, leadership development, competency development, and succession planning. More and more we see attempts to use tools for selection decisions and performance management. One caution light here is to ensure any assessment used is legally defensible. This can be a complex task to address.

Generally, the cognitive framework used in assessments focuses on the general intelligence or mental ability of a leader and how he or she might use that to analyze data and craft solutions. For example, Choices, a tool that measures "learning agility," looks at how people respond to changes and learn over time and offers perspective on an individual's people, results, mental, and change agility.

A different aspect of cognitive analysis yields multiple outputs around ambiguity, tolerance of uncertainty, and organization of complex information. It differs from cognitive "styles" for thinking and decision-making, which can be assessed by such tools as the MBTI. Having limited experience with cognitive complexity tools, I would describe those tools as helping to identify whether an individual looks at the complex or the simple and may be best used in selection or succession planning decisions.

Personality models attempt to provide individuals with insight into their needs, motivations, attitudes, and behavioral tendencies.

Assessing Emotional Intelligence

Emotional intelligence (EI) or emotional quota (EQ) assessments try to measure how individuals understand and respond to emotions. This connects with creating the kind of positive and trust-based work environment that fosters business results. EI tools generally attempt to assess: 1) ability to understand and explain emotions; 2) learned mental abilities or competencies for recognizing and understanding personal feelings and those of others; or 3) how an individual might cope with day-to-day situations.

The first approach, which is based on the research of two main psychology professors-Peter Salovey and John D. Mayer (who studied the ability to understand and use emotional information about social relationships), may attempt to measure emotional perceptions, understanding, and management.

The second approach, which is based on Daniel Goleman's model popularized in the 1990's would attempt to measure competencies such as empathy, self-awareness, motivation, social skills, and self-regulation. It is usually in the form of a 360 feedback tool.

The third model would be more like the personality traits and assess certain competencies such as general mood, how adaptable one is, intra and interpersonal skills, and how someone manages stress. Those types of assessments would be based on Bar-On's research and model of Emotional Intelligence from 1985 when Reuven Bar-On coined the term "EI".

In general, the types of EI and EQ competencies assessments try to measure things like assertiveness, confidence, happiness, empathy, self-awareness, impulse control, stress tolerance, interpersonal relations, motivation, and trust building abilities. Why? To help leaders have a positive emotional style that would foster the kind of work climate that leads to desired business outcomes. Often the successful executive profile includes components of empathy, self-awareness and assertiveness. Some scholars and practitioners believe these models and some tools are too broad and reliant on self-perception rather than actual skills of the leader.

Some organizations use cognitive ability tests for selection to assess general intelligence and seem to be less so for developmental reasons like coaching. More and more there seems to be a desire to use assessments for predicative reasons such as selection and succession. There seems to be a growing desire for data to justify or inform moves and promotions.

360 FEEDBACK AND ASSESSMENT

For me, the better assessment for the coaching client seems to be some form of qualitative 360 feedbacks where the comments are actionable items or suggestions.

When multi-rater tools are used that provide mostly numbers that reflect the average of how they rated on skills such as delegation or strategy, it may be easy for the organization to administer, however it can be more difficult for the developing leader to determine how to learn, grow, and change from being told they are a "5" or "2" in delegation. Just what does that mean and how does it help one change? The good news here is that it does provide data to explore when there are outliers on the tool with regard to the numbers. The numbers become grist for the mill and discussion items in coaching debriefs or application coaching.

Rich data around what the stakeholder's need, expect and suggest for the leaders or learner being assessed can be the most powerful data often found in the comment section of on-line 360 tools or gleaned from the coach doing stakeholder interviews. The real skill here is in the crafting of the right questions to ask to gather the key information that leads to behavior change. There are books written about how to custom design 360 feedback assessments.

OTHER ASSESSMENTS TO CONSIDER

The "Big Five" is another structure or model crafted in the 1930's by W. McDougall that relates to personality. R. Hogan's Hogan Personality Inventory uses six dimensions. These two models differ in language and definitions, but seem to look at similar and core personality dimensions that can be helpful to the coaching process and provide insight into impact on their direct reports, teams and the work. Here again, there are terms, language, and preferred personality profiles and traits that organizations need to consider which work or do not work given the culture they have or wish to create.

The personality models link desired traits to behaviors and make connections to how those can impact the performance of leaders. Examples of these assessments would be the 16PF and the MBTI. When using any of these, there are legal implications if used for selection. For coaching and development, when confidentiality is maintained and the goal is self-awareness, we still need to ensure we use valid and reliable surveys. Each of the tools we select is only as good as the extent to which they are used by the leader or learner to enhance their performance.

Color Q is an award-winning personality system, combining the work of the Myers-Briggs community, David Keirsey and modern day brain research. Designed to help individuals improve their leadership, team relationships and career development, it provides insights on four temperaments and their corresponding needs, values, talents and behaviors. Vivid and user friendly it is targeted to real life situations, easy to remember, highly accurate, and positive for all styles.

Table III contains more assessment tools to consider to find one that works for the coaching goal and aligns with the goals of the respective client organization.

TABLE III: OTHER ASSESSMENTS TO CONSIDER

ASSESSMENT	POTENTIAL USE	CONTACT INFORMATION
Maturity Assessment Profile (MAP) Or Leadership Development Profile (LDP)	To assess current stage of adult development to craft an individual development plan	Cook-Creuter Researchers
The Leadership Circle Profile	For both 360 feedback and related belief systems that may impede the full use of competencies aligned with Senge's model	Leadershipcircle.com

The Forte Communication Style System	To measure communication styles on four scales: dominance, extraversion, patience and conformity	Theforteinstitute.com
Opq32 Occupational Personality Questionnaire Or EI Report Pack	Tailored to different job levels to diagnosis and predict the overall emotional skills at work (EI)	SHL
Firo B	To identify our unique needs that motivate us in the areas of inclusion, control and affection	CPP Inc Publishers
The Winslow Reports Assessment Suite	To measure behavior and personality; interpersonal, organizational, dedication, and self-control traits	Andi Roberts
Personal Communication Style Inventory (PCSI)	Communication styles	Peggy Grall and Associates
Kolb Learning Styles	Understand four learning styles: accommodating, converging, diverging, and assimilating	David A. Kolb Model
16personality Factor (16PF) Questionnaire	To support vocational guidance, hiring and promotional recommendations	Pearson Assessments by Raymond B. Cattell
Color Q	To provide insight on four temperaments and corresponding needs, values, talents and behaviors.	Color Qpersonalities. com or Zichy@earthlink. net

By way of example, here is a story about how, as an internal coach, an assessment tool was used to enhance collaboration and resolve conflict between peers.

USING ASSESSMENT TO RESOLVE CONFLICT AND ENHANCE COLLABORATION:

A STORY

When a leader approached the coaching practitioner she was frustrated with two newly promoted leaders under her supervision who needed to work well together to accomplish complex goals under very tight deadlines. Although both were strong producers and committed to excellence, they could have produced greater results if they would collaborate more and seemed to be getting in each other's way. The coach listened and offered to help resolve the conflict by meeting with each one separately and then together.

When he met with one new leader, he realized her preference for gathering data was for detail and her tendencies were for perfection. As an introvert, she often reached out to her peer leader via email to request data needed to complete reports.

The other leader had gathered data differently. Her preference was for using a more intuitive process, hunch, or theme gathered by her extroverted style. She had much experience and believed the peer did not respect her contribution. The peer wanted to get it right and focused on the details. She wanted to get it done and look at the implications and the big picture.

After doing their Myers-Briggs Type Indicators, they both realized that their styles were very different. Not only did they have different styles, but were polar opposites on the indicator. When they appreciated the other person's style as just different, together their product was so much better. They had to learn to value each other's contribution and styles before they could work well together.

Seeing the differences, and well-indented styles, they found a more productive way to have both the details and the themes and to get it right and get it done in a more collaborative way. They might not get along, but with common goals and an appreciation of style preferences they now communicate better as they jointly produce documents and get results.

SUMMARY

From an internal or external coaching perspective, the key takeaways are clear on the why and how's of any assessment tool or practice. Let the driver be the coaching agenda. Do not use or allow others to use tools they are not trained or certified to use. Be aware of the implications for the client and the client organization. It is not a toy or about what the stars have in store for you this month.

Be aware of the costs and confidentiality. Make sure there is a good business reason for using the tool and that you did your homework about the integrity of the tool itself and what it attempts to measure or predict. In short, do not try this at home or while driving heavy machinery. It is both and art and a science. Get educated and trained before use.

Kathryn Wankel is an independent executive coach and senior facilitator. Prior to having her own coaching practice, she served as an internal executive coach, a human resource professional, and a talent and leadership development leader in the financial services industry in New York City. Educated at Columbia University, her focus has been on executive and organizational coaching and leadership development.

9

Multi-Rater Feedback in Executive Coaching Engagements: An Exploration of Best Practices

By Dr. Rachel Ciporen

INTRODUCTION:

In 2014 the idea that continuous learning is necessary for organizations to compete in our diverse, complex, and constantly evolving marketplace is well accepted. Approaches to helping executives meet the expanding requirements of their role as they move through various leadership transitions are getting extensive attention. Increasingly, 360 Degree Feedback (also known as multi-rater feedback) is used as a way to help leaders understand how various stakeholders view their performance in comparison to set competency measures. 360 Degree Feedback has the potential to increase self-awareness, prompt transformative learning (as a result of disconnects between how one sees oneself and how one is seen by others), as well as provide insight into blind spots in performance and impact. However, the process also has the potential to create resentment, decrease motivation, cause data-overload and "survey fatigue", as well as waste money (if a process isn't in place to support leaders in making changes based on identified areas for development). This chapter provides an overview of best practices and key considerations for Human Resource, Talent Management, and Organizational Development professionals as well as executives and external & internal coaches to consider when evaluating or developing their approach to 360-coaching.

As noted in the previous chapter by Wankel, assessments are utilized extensively in executive and organizational coaching engagements, and 360-Degree Feedback assessments are one of the most frequently used types of assessments (Sherpa Executive Coaching Survey, 2012). After development-focused coaching, 360-coaching was identified as the most frequently used type of coaching engagement by both external and internal coaches responding to the 2010 Conference Board Survey. While 360-Degree Feedback is widely used in organizations, there are multiple approaches to critical aspects of its use and administration, which this chapter will discuss.

To capture current best practices in designing and implementing 360 feedback processes, I interviewed thirteen Columbia Coaching Certification Program trained coaches who use 360 Degree Feedback in organizations. Of the thirteen, six work as internal coaches at companies representing a diversity of industries including financial services, personal care, retail, pharmaceuticals and mining; the remaining seven work as external coaches with assignments across multiple industries and in a combination of large multi-national corporations and smaller enterprises. In order to capture some of the diversity that exists regionally, I interviewed coaches who are based and have extensive experience in Brazil, Canada, China, India, Switzerland, and the United States. Findings from this diverse albeit small sample reveals the efficacy of particular trends in 360 Degree Feedback across cultural and organizational contexts. I am grateful for interview participants' expertise and insights, which have informed the sections that follow.

This chapter addresses the following key issues related to 360-Degree Feedback:

- Understanding the best types of 360 Degree Feedback Reports for a given context (including customized organizational competencies, off the shelf surveys, and stakeholder interviews)

- Assessing Readiness for 360-Degree Feedback (at the organizational and individual level)

- Confidentiality

- Cultural Differences

- A System's Approach to 360 Degree Feedback

- Best Practices

TYPES OF 360 DEGREE FEEDBACK

360-Degree surveys and stakeholder interviews provide coachees with important insights into how they are perceived by a broader segment of the organization beyond what is afforded by the traditional manager-only review process. Because a leader's success is often measured by the accomplishments of her team and peers' perceptions often impact a leader's reputation and subsequent career mobility, the insights that can be gained through this broader data is often invaluable. All of the coaches interviewed for this chapter identified "helping clients identify blind-spots" as the most important contribution of the reports. Gosia a successful external coach with extensive experience across Asia and Europe, explains "360s can create positive shock for executives who without firm data, deny their behavior is creating any negative impact on others." As Robert Hargrove (2003) notes in his book "Masterful Coaching", a key role of a coach is to help clients limit defensive routines that interrupt their ability to adapt and innovate outside of their habitual patterns. 360 and multi-stakeholder feedback can help leaders see that "despite their good intentions, they often produce unintended consequences due to lack of awareness" (pg. 181).

Marcelo, an internal coach in Brazil describes the changes he is seeing as 360-coaching is used more widely organization. He states "They are growing into leaders. What we had in the past were managers of businesses. Through the 360 they realized that, 'hey, I have to deal with people. Now someone is talking to me about my career development and my blind spots and it feels good. Maybe I can do that for my team too'. You see a different guy. They have a whole new level to play with 'I can make a difference in people's lives.' I have seen five people get promoted because of the work they did as a result of 360-coaching they received. These leaders are now disseminating the culture."

Of the coaches interviewed for this chapter, almost all used some type of 360 or multi-stakeholder interview process in the majority of their coaching engagements. In large scale coaching initiatives coaches frequently employed survey reports customized to particular organizational competency models, both during leadership development programs and to inform ongoing coaching engagements. In these cases coaches reported spending 1-4 hours debriefing the reports and all assisted clients to develop action plans based on the feedback.

Meanwhile, several organizations utilized qualitative interviews instead of online surveys, especially when coaching engagements were at higher levels in the organization. While qualitative interviews are more expensive and time-consuming, both internal and external coaches tended to see interviews as providing a more nuanced look into a coachee's strengths and areas for development. Further, by building rapport with feedback providers and personally committing to keeping the confidentiality of the interviewee's comments, many coaches found they were able to get richer data than from a survey alone. Gopal, an external coach with a successful practice based in India that works with large multinationals across multiple continents, notes that "Often, it is what is left unsaid that speaks louder than what is said... The art of the 360 is to read between the lines." As this comment illustrates, qualitative interviewing allows for more nuance in the feedback than a traditional survey allows, but requires skill and training to execute well.

There was a range of perspectives on how often 360 Degree Feedback should be collected. In order to determine if an organization was seeing results from a coaching engagement, some coaches began conversations with key-stakeholders several months after initiating an action plan with their client. Others worked in organizations where 360 Degree Feedback was a yearly event tied to the formal performance review process and used previous reports to gauge change. Jay, an internal coach based in the United States who works at Zoetis, warns, "Be judicious—people can be surveyed to death. Use them sparingly."

ASSESSING READINESS FOR 360 DEGREE FEEDBACK

A critical success factor for any 360-process is to first assess the readiness of the organization and individual. The value of 360 Degree Feedback is dependent on both the feedback providers' ability to articulate what is working and what most needs to be improved for the leader to be successful in their role. Also, the leader must to be open to the feedback and willing to change. As with any other leadership development initiative, its value is heavily impacted by how it is introduced and supported within the organization. As one of the internal coaches interviewed for this article noted, for a 360 initiative to be successful it needs to a) be linked to business strategy, b) have executive sponsorship, and c) be part of a well thought-out process that links to key business challenges. Organizations where there is a low degree of trust or employees have limited training and ability to provide constructive feedback are not good candidates for 360 Degree Feedback. Similarly, leaders who demonstrate openness to feedback and a willingness to accept challenge as well as support are more likely to derive benefit from an organization's investment in 360-coaching than leaders who feel they already know it all.

The importance of organizational readiness was brought home to me several years ago when I was hired to help a company design a leadership development program with a 360 Degree Feedback component for their director level leaders.   The leadership program was going well; however, when it came to debriefing the 360 Degree Feedback reports we found that they lacked substance with most raters choosing "average" scores on all competency measures and not completing the qualitative comments section.   In the few places where leaders were given constructive feedback, the leader's reaction was frequently one of anger and wanting to find out "who said that?" With the support of my internal OD partner (who had only been at the organization for six months when we began this initiative) we began to have informal conversations with employees who had been asked to provide feedback. We learned through those conversations that there had been a similar feedback initiative several years earlier and that anonymity had not been protected. Several employees had found themselves very isolated politically and several people ended up quitting or getting fired.

It took my internal OD partner several years to build a reputation of trustworthiness within the broader organization and it was only once that trust was established that he re-instated the 360 Degree Feedback reports and coaching into the leadership development program. During those several years HR and OD did a lot of work with the leadership, introducing research on emotional intelligence and the importance of self-awareness (and feedback's role in developing self-awareness) to help develop the leaders' readiness to accept and work with feedback. They also introduced Marshall Goldsmith's concept of "Feed forward" and used his framing that feedback is "a gift". Simultaneously they created workshops on providing constructive feedback to help employees at all levels better communicate their experience of what was working, what a leader could improve, and what they could change.

The 360-coaching sessions are now one of the highest scoring elements of the leadership development program and the organization is promoting more internal leaders (vs. hiring externally for higher level positions) than ever before. The rich feedback that the leaders are now receiving (and taking in) has led to both better performance and a more positive organizational climate as evidenced by positive change scores on employee engagement surveys. This story highlights the importance of organizational readiness as a critical factor in the success of 360 Degree Feedback.

CONFIDENTIALITY

There is still a great deal of variation on how organizations use 360s; for some it's an evaluation tool where scores are linked to employee satisfaction surveys and other performance metrics, or used as part of a talent review process. In other organizations 360 Degree Feedback is used for purely developmental purposes. While many of the coaches interviewed for this study noted using the 360 Degree Feedback as part of a performance review, the majority felt that it was best leveraged for development. This distinction has an important implication, of course; when a 360 is used as a pure development tool, the coach and coachee are typically the only people who will see the report. While coachees are often encouraged to share major themes and elements of their action plan, they have ultimate control over what is shared from the report and with whom. This approach builds trust and empowerment through having the coachee communicate their learning and action plans vs. having the coach speak on their behalf. The role of the coach in these meetings is one of facilitator vs. presenter.

When 360s are used as part of performance evaluation or talent review, a wider internal audience sees the results. While it is easy to make the case for the value of sharing the data for a talent review process, the potential downsides (political maneuvering, sanitized feedback, anxiety, scapegoating, decreased intimacy in the coaching relationship due to trying to look "good") seem to suggest that the use of 360-data as part of a performance evaluation process should only be undertaken in organizations with sophisticated learning and development practices and well developed and articulated coaching processes and procedures led by a knowledgeable internal sponsor with sufficient positional power to manage the process with continuous attention to ethics. Bob, Director of Executive Coaching at Gap Inc., advocates that in a talent review process "The results of these assessments (including 360s) are just one piece of the puzzle; by no means do you make a talent decision based on one of them." In some organizations with robust internal coaching practices, the actual feedback report is not shared with the broader organization, but the coach will still share their perspective of the leader during a talent review session.

Several of the coaches who I interviewed that do extensive international work noted that conceptions of confidentiality vary widely from country to country. Similarly the word "confidential" means different things to different people. One external coach recalled an early coaching engagement where he promised his client: "I will keep what you tell me confidential". About halfway through the process the HR sponsor asked for a progress report on the engagement and the coach shared his perceptions of the client while being careful to not to share any of the client's specific words or phrases. When the client found out that the coach had shared his perceptions of her with the HR sponsor she felt that confidentiality had been breached and the relationship never recovered. For the coach, not sharing her words was keeping confidentiality; for the coachee, sharing his perceptions of her based on her words went against the intent of confidentiality. He learned the hard way the importance of being very explicit about what "confidentiality" means.

CULTURAL DIFFERENCES

One's beliefs about many of the topics discussed earlier in this chapter (the importance of direct communication, ethics, performance, confidentiality, approach to hierarchy, etc.) are mediated by our national, functional (sales, research, etc), industry, and organizational cultures. While it is outside of the scope of this article to go into detail about the ways in which culture impacts 360-coaching, I would be remiss not to briefly highlight the profound ways these differences can emerge in cross-cultural coaching engagements and for leaders operating in cross-cultural business environments. For further reading on the intersection of coaching and culture readers may want to explore Philippe Rosinski's book "Coaching Across Cultures: New Tools for Leveraging National, Corporate & Professional Differences." There are also several assessments (including ITAP International's Culture in the Workplace Questionnaire) that can provide a window into various dimensions of culture that are often at play in cross-cultural business exchanges.

A System's Approach to 360-Coaching

Kurt Lewin's famous equation that "behavior is a function of the person and the environment" ($B=f(P,E)$) is an important reminder for coaches. It is easy to see a 360-report and focus only on the person in front of you when in reality, the organizational context and culture has enormous influence on how an individual leader behaves and performs. When debriefing a 360-report, especially if you are an external coach, it is useful to begin the debrief by asking the coachee what important contextual factors you should know about their organization (lay-offs, merger, new boss, new role, etc.) as well as any important personal factors that may be influencing their performance (illness, a new baby, taking care of elderly parents, etc.) along with their particular business challenges and objectives. Similarly, it is useful when introducing a 360-process to an organization to educate feedback providers that the purpose of the feedback is to help the leader become even more successful in their role and to prepare them that they will not see change overnight. When I conduct multi-stakeholder interviews I end the interview by asking what the interviewee can do to support the leader's growth towards the development goals they have just identified. This helps keep the interviews from devolving into venting sessions and puts responsibility on all members of the system to work towards the desired change.

Best Practices and Things to Watch Out For:

Best Practices for 360 Degree Feedback Coaching
• Learn about the organizational context the coachee is operating in. What is considered successful leadership behavior varies greatly across industries and cultures.
• Allow space for coachee to process emotional reactions to feedback.
• Learn the feedback tool you will be debriefing inside and out. You will be expected to answer questions about the assessment you are administering.
• For internal coaches: be explicit when you are coaching vs. Interacting from a different role.

• Present strengths as well as areas for improvement whenever delivering feedback.
• Be explicit about the terms of confidentiality – who will the report be shared with and how will it be used? Transparency builds trust.
• Protect the privacy of those providing feedback. If qualitative comments will be presented verbatim, make sure raters know that before they share their comments.
• Help coachee develop an action plan based on the feedback report. Insight without a clear action plan is often not sufficient for lasting behavior change. Help the coachee decide on timelines and resources for support.
• Assist the coachee to connect their action plan to key business goals and personal values.
• For HR and talent management sponsors: review the list of colleagues a leader is requesting feedback from to ensure a representative sample.
• Encourage coachees to thank everyone who provided feedback and share elements of their action plan as appropriate.
• Look for opportunities to provide challenge as well as support.
• For internal coaches: providing challenge can be difficult when coaching leaders at higher levels in the organization – if you feel that your approach as a coach will be limited by the organizational hierarchy think about partnering with an external coach.
• Obtain executive sponsorship for any coaching initiative. Invite the executive team to model openness to feedback and behavior change.
• Take a systems perspective – the coachee's behavior is influenced by their personality, skills, values and mindset, but also by the organizational norms, values, reward systems and expectations. An effective coaching engagement acknowledges both yet helps the coachee focus on what is within his or her ability to change or leverage.

- Put responsibility on all parties. Educate feedback providers to look at their role in the positive or negative dynamic they are commenting on. Encourage respondents to look for evidence that the coachee is attempting to change and reinforce positive behaviors.

- Assist the coachee in making personal meaning of the feedback rather than explaining or telling. This increases commitment and engagement.

- When introducing 360 or multi-stakeholder feedback processes into your organization, provide training to feedback providers who may not have the necessary skills to provide constructive and usable insights

- Be aware of cultural differences – for example, expectations regarding direct vs. Indirect communication vary widely – recognize your own cultural norms and seek to understand how that may or may not be aligned with the national and organizational culture within which you or your coachee are operating.

WHAT TO AVOID DURING 360 DEGREE COACHING

- Do not assist your coachee in looking for who to blame for "bad" results or comments. While hurt feelings and anger are a normal part of the process, the coach should take steps to ensure that no retaliatory action or blaming conversations take place after the 360-debrief. Failure to do so can have a lasting impact on how people participate in the 360s and on your own reputation.

- Never share elements of the feedback report without explicit contract to do so. Trust takes time to build and only seconds to destroy.

- Avoid a data-driven approach without empathy for the personal impact of the feedback.

• Try to prevent survey fatigue. The quality of the feedback you provide is impacted by the number of concurrent initiatives in the organization. Timing matters both to the coachee and the respondents.
• Avoid triangulation – whenever possible have the coachee share themes from the feedback and aspects of their action plan directly with his or her manager or HR sponsor rather than having the coach speak on the coachee's behalf. This generates trust and a sense of empowerment.

SUMMARY

360 Degree Feedback has enormous potential to raise self-awareness and be a positive catalyst for behavior change. By learning about their impact on others, many leaders go on to create positive climate shifts in their teams and broader organizations. As many of the coaches I interviewed note, leaders may also get the personal benefit of promotions and improved reputations. Because many organizational cultures are conflict averse, 360-Degree Feedback is often the only source of honest detailed feedback that leaders get from their peers and direct reports. Many leaders report gaining critical insights into developmental needs based on the feedback. At the same time, fear of retaliation, political maneuvering, and lack of feedback skills can make the information obtained during 360 Degree Feedback interviews or surveys close to useless or potentially harmful. Similarly, poorly planned 360-initiatves can lead to survey fatigue among respondents and "data overload" for leaders who can become desensitized by overexposure to assessments and new leadership initiatives. As a coach or 360-coaching organizational sponsor there is much work to do before you begin the 360-initiative to make sure the organization and the leader are ready to utilize the feedback in a way that provides measurable results and a real return on investment.

REFERENCES:

Hargrove, R. (2003). Masterful Coaching: Inspire an "Impossible Future" While Producing Extraordinary Leaders and Extraordinary Results. San Francisco: Jossey-Bass/Pfeiffer.

Rosinski, P. (2003). Coaching Across Cultures: New Tools for Leveraging National, Corporate, and Professional Differences. Boston: Nicholas Brealey Publishing.

Sherpa Coaching, (2012) Seventh Annual Executive Coaching Survey. http://www.sherpacoaching.com/survey.html

Silvert, H.M., Wanveer, L., Pomerleau, M. (2010) The Conference Board. 2010 Executive Coaching Survey: A Summary of Key Executive Coaching Practices. http://www.conference-board.org/publications/publicationdetail.cfm?publicationid=1768&subtopicid=170

Thach, E.C. (2002). The Impact of Executive Coaching and 360 Feedback on Leadership Effectiveness. Leadership and Organizational Development Journal. 23 (4), 205-214.

Rachel Ciporen works with global executives across multiple industries and has coached over a thousand leaders to successfully respond to strategic business challenges. In addition to her private consulting practice Rachel is a core faculty member in the Columbia University Coaching Certification Program and the Gestalt Organization and Systems Development Center. She has coached in in Columbia Business School's Executive Education programs since 2004. Rachel received her doctorate in Adult Learning and Leadership and her Masters in Organizational Psychology from Teachers College, Columbia University. She is a Board Certified Coach through the Center for Credentialing and Education. Rachel's research on leadership development, executive education, and transformative learning have appeared in several journals including The Academy of Management Learning and Education, The Journal of Leadership & Organizational Studies, and The Journal for Action Research. She is certified in numerous assessment tools including: Culture in the Workplace, EQi 2, The Hogan Assessment Suite, and the Neethling Brain Inventory (NBI).

How Executive Coaching Helps Businesses Transform

By Stefan Hendriks

INTRODUCTION

With an increasingly connected and globalizing economy, transformations are becoming daily practice for many companies. As a consultant, my role in the transformations is to assist with change management strategies. The main components of a change strategy are stakeholder management, communications and training. One component related to stakeholder management and communications is to create a network of influential executives (called change leaders), who actively support and advocate for the strategic direction and vision of the business transformation. These change leaders are usually influential people who are well respected in the organization and are able to convincingly articulate a vision and bring people along with it.

I hadn't thought about including executive coaching into the change network, until I started leading a leadership development program for one of my clients. The program included both mentors and executive coaches. Since I had no experience with executive coaches, my boss suggested obtaining a certification in executive coaching. During the Columbia Coaching Certification Program (CCCP), I started to wonder why I had never used executive coaches in my change strategies. After completion of the Columbia Coaching Certification Program, Dr. Anne Power, CCCP faculty, approached me about writing a chapter in this book and we agreed to explore how Executive Coaching could contribute to business success by including executive coaches into a change management strategy.

The first part of the chapter presents definitions and concepts for change management and executive coaching to set a foundation for this chapter and create a common language. The second part describes the approach to answer the following two questions:

1. **How can executive coaches contribute to business success?**

2. **How does an ideal coaching engagement - with the goal to support executives in business transformations - look like?**

Six executives were interviewed with the above questions in a global Consumer Goods company in the spring of 2013. The results are presented in the third section of the chapter. The results of the interviews were compared and contrasted to extract themes. They were compared with the following sources of information:

1. **Notes of the interviews**

2. **CCCP competencies and CCCP coaching process**

3. **My experience as a consultant and coach**

The chapter concludes with a summary and recommendations for practice and future research.

Definitions of Change Management and Executive Coaching

Definition of Change Management

The approach for change management I use in my work as a change management consultant is the approach created by Kotter (1995, 2002, 2007). Kotter wrote several articles on change management in the Harvard Business Review, culminating in a book titled: The Heart of Change. Kotter defines change management as: "The utilization of basic structures and tools to control any organizational change effort. Change management's goal is to minimize the change impacts on workers and avoid distractions." His most important message is that people primarily change resulting from an emotional reaction to a suggested change, be it a different vision, operating model, process, technology or a way of doing things. He argues that visualizing change in a way that speaks to people's emotions will increase the likelihood of people supporting the change and act on it. This is a different message than what many of us have seen in the corporate world, where often transformations are presented in a rational fashion with facts and statistics (we all have seen the presentations with the numbers and the graphs). There are eight steps in Kotter's change model.

Kotter's first step is to create a sense of urgency for the business transformation. Without a sense of urgency, people aren't necessarily compelled to change. The sense of urgency can come from a variety of sources. Pain is the most powerful source of urgency. Showing people that something is wrong with the current state of your business (bleeding money, broken processes, inefficiencies in people's daily work) is a good way to instill a sense of urgency in people. Other sources of urgency are new business opportunities or competitive forces in the industry.

The second step is to create a guiding coalition of people, including advocates, change leaders and team members with the right combination of technical skills and people skills. This team of people will create a vision for the transformation (third step). A vision is what the end state of the transformation will look like. This step is a crucial part in any transformation. In many cases, people start projects and transformations without a clear vision in mind. Forming the guiding coalition comes before creating the vision. The rationale is because a team has to develop, agree and commit to the vision to create the necessary buy in to move forward with the group.

Even more important is the fourth step: communicating the vision through every possible channel. Here leadership behaviors become crucial and executive coaching can play an important role. If leaders display behaviors which go against what the new vision is trying to achieve, people will be hesitant to change.

The remaining steps are removing barriers to success (organization structure changes, bosses who live in the old world, etc.), communicating short term wins, sustaining momentum and making sure the changes stick. Change leaders play a role in all these steps, but their role is most visible in setting and communicating the new direction.

DEFINITION OF COACHING

The International Coaching Federation (ICF) has a definition of coaching which is used by the Columbia Coaching Certification Program is: "Coaching is partnering with clients in a thought-provoking and creative process that inspires them to maximize their personal and professional potential."

The ICF further describes coaching with the following statements:

- "Coaches provide an ongoing partnership designed to help clients produce fulfilling results in their personal and professional lives. Coaches help people improve their performances and enhance the quality of their lives."

- "Coaches are trained to listen, to observe and to customize their approach to individual client needs. They seek to elicit solutions and strategies from the client; they believe the client is naturally creative and resourceful. The coach's job is to provide support to enhance the skills, resources and creativity that the client already has."

Both the change management and coaching definitions were presented to the executives at the start of the interview.

APPROACH

To answer the first question of how executive coaching can contribute to successful business transformations, six executives were interviewed in a global consumer goods company. All executives were key players (change leaders) in a variety of business transformations which were either completed or still ongoing at the time of the interviews. None of the executives had a coach during the business transformations. The executives worked on the following transformations:

- Global HR transformation and systems implementation, including Shared Services, Centers of Expertise and global processes and systems

- HRMS System implementation in Europe & the Middle East

- (Re) – Integration of the bottler organization into the parent company

- Opening of a warehouse and manufacturing facility in Las Vegas

The semi structured interviews took place over the phone or in person.

After personal introductions and the review of the definitions of both change management and executive coaching, I asked the executives the following questions:

1. **What value does executive coaching bring to executives who are responsible for large scale business transformations?**

2. **How does a coaching engagement for a large scale business transformation look like with regards to a number of design elements?**

For question # 2, the following design elements were presented to the executives:

- *Voluntary or mandatory nature of the coaching relationship*: is the coaching relationship voluntary or mandatory? Mandatory includes active participation and consequences for non-participation.

- *Standard or customized coaching program*: Do all participants receive an equal program or is the coaching relationship designed around the business transformation?

- *External or internal coach*: Which coach is better suited to assist an executive with a business transformation?

- What are characteristics of effective change leaders and coaches?

- *Length of the program*: What is the ideal length of a coaching engagement during a transformation?

- *Coaching or mentoring*: What type of coaching is best suited to help change leaders during a transformation?

- *Timing of coaching*: During what time of the business transformation is coaching most appropriate?

Notes from all the interviews were analyzed for common themes and interesting perspectives from the interviewers to show a variety of opinions on the questions. I also looked for opinions which could add new angles, perspectives to the field of executive coaching and change management.

RESULTS

The results are presented in two sections. The first section discusses the results from the first question. The second section discusses the results of the second question. I compare the results with concepts and theories of coaching from the Columbia Coaching Certification program to see if the models and concepts are confirmed by what the interviewees said. I make comments about the results based on my experience as a change consultant and executive coach.

Question 1: What value does executive coaching bring to executives who are responsible for large scale business transformations?

THEMES

1. Coaching helps to realize the Vision

Step three and step four in the Kotter model are creating and communicating the vision to ensure the success of a transformation. The statements of the interviewees confirm that 1. Creating and communicating a vision is essential for success and, 2. An executive coach is able to assist a change leader in realizing the vision of the transformation.

One executive said that executive coaching helps the executive with realizing the vision of the transformation. There is usually a vision at the start of a transformation which is translated into a project plan and a budget. But when the project is underway, it is easy to forget what the initial vision of the project was. "It is very easy to lose sight of the vision and objectives of the project," said the same interviewee. The executive further described how the lack of focus on the vision resulted in a failed implementation, even though the users were ready to use the system. He explained that during the design and construction phase of the system, little time was used to exploit the functionality of the system to improve the productivity, efficiency and competitiveness of the company. All the focus was on getting the users ready to use the system. If people forget about the vision, or if it is not articulated to project team-members and end users, often an organization ends up recreating the current state with a new system, wasting millions of dollars in the process. The strategic objectives set out at the start of the project take a backseat to the budget and the project plan. In my practice as a consultant, I have seen this happen countless times. Executives get stuck in the middle of driving the vision and the business case and pleasing stakeholders who oppose to the new vision, or settle for something that is a weak version of the vision, as long as it gets implemented to claim success. There is a tradeof to be made between realizing the full vision at once or implementing the vision in smaller increments. It is sometimes easier for people to dea with incremental changes and it is less risky. But this tradeoff is not the same as giving up on the vision or not realizing the benefits of the vision due to budgetary and time pressures.

In summary, an executive coach can help the Change Leader to realize the vision of the transformation and realize the Return of Investment set out in the Business Case of the Transformation. The coach can help the Change Leader to track the benefits of the business case and constantly remind the leader where he/she is with the realization of the vision and encourage the executive to not let go of the vision.

CCCP Competencies which help executives with realizing the vision of the business transformation

The goal of looking at the CCCP competencies is to see which competencies are most helpful for coaches to coach executives with the realization of the vision of the business transformation. The CCCP teaches nine coaching competencies: relating, coaching presence leveraging diversity, questioning, listening, testing assumptions reframing, contributing and business acumen

The competencies are divided in three categories, each representing an aspect of the coaching relationship. One category has competencies for building the relationship with the coachee, a prerequisite for any successful coaching to occur; the second category helps coachees make meaning of what they are doing and the third category helps coachees take action. At the category level, the competencies associated with the category making meaning and helping the coachee succeed are key to assisting the executives with the realization of the vision.

Looking at the individual competencies within the categories, testing assumptions, reframing and business acumen are necessary to assist the executives in realizing their visions. I have often seen leaders operate with a single set of assumptions driving their behavior. They often get focused on "getting it done." Due to the budget pressures and deadlines, they develop a low tolerance and patience for different points of view, objections and questions from stakeholders and people impacted by the transformation. They don't understand why people have objections to their great ideas. Testing assumptions will help an executive solidify the strength of the vision and be able to better articulate it to multiple audiences who test and question the vision.

Reframing is useful during the creation of the vision. Through reframing, a vision can be created by looking at multiple perspectives and how this can contribute to a richer and informed vision. One of the characteristics of a vision is whether it is achievable (Kotter, 2007). Considering multiple perspectives through reframing will make the vision more achievable.

Business Acumen as a competency is a pre-requisite to be successful as an executive coach in this context. The field of executive coaching debates this issue at great length (whether a coach must have similar industry experience as the coachee). One side of the argument claims that an executive coach does not need to have experience in the business or industries their clients operate. The other side claims that an executive coach can only help a coachee effectively if the coach understands the business and industry of their clients. In my experience as a coach, regardless of what side of the debate you are on, clients, HR and managers will select coaches for executives with a combination of industry, functional and sometimes even role experience.

2. Executive coaching increases self-awareness

One interviewee described a situation where a newly appointed leader had a leadership style unfit for the company's project culture, affecting the project's team culture and performance negatively. The interviewee was the overall project leader of the transformation. He decided to appoint an internal coach to assist the new leader with improving his leadership style and self-awareness.

The executive coach collected information from the leader's manager and the people around him (360 Feedback) and discussed the results with the leader to create insights and awareness. The biggest behavioral issues from the 360 feedback results were collaborative decision making and sharing of information to all project members. After analyzing and discussing the results, both coach and the leader defined behavioral objectives. These behaviors were tracked by the coach and discussed with the leader during a number of coaching sessions.

The results made an impact. The leader improved his leadership skills by being more collaborative and sharing information with all team-members. The project was completed successfully within time and budget. The interviewee mentioned a similar example in which an external coach was appointed to help a project leader to be more collaborative and inclusive with the members of the team.

I am making a side-step to explain the CCCP coaching process here after which I will apply it to the above situation. The CCCP coaching process consists of three phases: context, content and conduct. During the first phase, the coach explores the context with the coachee and contracts with the coachee about the coaching situation or opportunity. In addition the coach discusses with the coachee what information sources will be consulted to understand where the coachee is with regards to the coaching situation. The second phase, the content phase, focuses on analyzing the feedback and exploring options, selecting viable options and planning for the selected option (s). In the last phase, coaches assist the executive with experimentation and integrating new behaviors into the daily lives of the executives. For a business transformation, the coaching process shifts from personal to organizational. The coach and the executive agree on what is needed for individual *and* organizational success.

Applying the CCCP coaching process to the previous situation described by the interviewee, the engagement focused on Situation Analysis and Feedback and moved into the planning of actions and the monitoring of the results. Entry and contracting wasn't part of the process. The leader didn't have much choice. The engagement was mandated in the context of his role. There wasn't also much freedom for the leader to explore opportunities and determine which path to follow.

In a business a transformation, the coaching process must be adapted to fit the context of the transformation. The focus shifts from the individual developmental opportunities of the coachee to the goals of the transformation. The executive becomes a vehicle of the transformation; the coachee is not the main focus of the coaching engagement. This is difference with how both the definition of the ICF and the coaching process are framed and described.

3. Coaching helps executives learn

Often leaders are given the responsibility to lead projects or play an important change leadership role, based on their successes in the past or their abilities to be a leader. However, in many cases, the new role requires new competencies and skills. A coach can help a leader gain new competencies to be successful in their new job as a change leader.

One interviewee gave the example of opening a new manufacturing plant in Las Vegas. He was appointed as the HR executive to help open the facility. Shortly after the interviewee started working, the general manager left the company and he was left to his own devices. He had to find out many things on his own. It was a very stressful time for him and a very risky situation for the consumer goods company. It wasn't until the arrival of a VP of HR and a new general manager, that they were able to form a team who successfully opened the new facility. According to the interviewee, a coach could have helped him learn the ropes of the job.

I think in his situation, a mentor with functional knowledge would have been a better fit than a coach. He was relatively inexperienced as an executive with opening a facility of this size. There is a difference between coaching and mentoring. Coaching sets specific goals and is focused on changing someone's behavior. The functional skills aren't a primary focus of the engagement. Mentoring has a long term focus and the relationship is based on professional development. A mentor is usually someone who has a similar background and skillset as the mentee. The mentee learns from his mentor because of his expertise and experience. There is less pressure and mentees can consult with the mentor, yet still make decisions which are best for their career.

When selecting a coach for senior leaders during a transformation, a coach with both coaching and mentoring skills is ideal. Coaching skills help the client to be a successful change leader. Coach and executive can work on competencies such as executive presence, bringing people along, communication, collaboration and incorporating various perspectives into the vision. Experience in the field and the situation (mentoring skills) help the executive to accelerate the learning and to achieve deadlines and goals. A transformation usually has a predefined set of financial objectives and a timeline, which become part of a senior leader's executive compensation package. An executive will look for a coach who can help to achieve the performance goals.

The interviewee gave a perfect example of someone who had a hybrid of coaching and mentoring skills. The new VP of HR helped the interviewee with a set of skills (staffing/hiring, HR processes, Benefits and Compensation and Organization Design) while letting him experiment with new approaches (coaching skills).

Interviewees also mentioned the benefits of having a coach to help build confidence to learn and be successful in the role.

4.   Executive Coaching helps to navigate Relationships

Relationships are critical to the leader's success throughout the transformation. One interviewee described a situation in which he was appointed to manage the integration of the bottler organization into the parent company. The consumer goods company sold the bottler organization 10 years ago to maximize the profitability of both organizations. After 10 years, the board decided to merge the bottler organization back into the company to create synergies between manufacturing and distribution.

Soon after the kickoff of the project, the relationships between the bottler organization and the parent company became tense. Much was at stake for the people involved. During the split, the bottler organization created its own infrastructure and processes to support the business. The bottler organization had to abandon the infrastructure and adopt the infrastructure of the parent company. Many jobs were on the line and leaders were jockeying for positions. The interviewee discussed how he was not prepared for this situation and how he was not equipped to deal with the power struggles and the conflicts. He opined that a coach would have helped him navigate the relationships and handle the conflicts better. He suggested coaches for all executives involved in the transformation to help navigate the web of relationships.

5.   Coaching helps to create and sustain a culture of success

When people come together to deliver a transformation, it is not a given that the project will be a success. People usually come from different backgrounds, have different sets of skills and – in coaching terms – have different frames of references. One interviewee gave the example of a transformation project where they built a common culture based on the principles of the Speed of Trust (Covey, 2006). One of Covey's main messages is that trust among team members has a positive impact on many things (e. g. cost reduction, speed of implementation). The consumer goods company created an internal program for project teams to go through a workshop based on Covey's trust principles and process. After the team went through the workshop, coaching was used to reinforce the behaviors and help the team with driving consensus in decision making.

6. Coaching creates a safe environment

Coaching offers a safe environment to the executives and change leaders. One way is to provide moral support to the executives and change leaders. One interviewee said that it can be lonely and contentious at times. Dealing with the amount of change and everything being in a state of flux, support is needed to keep believing in yourself as a leader and in your capacity to successfully lead through a transformation. One interviewee said: "It would be so nice to have a coach to support me in my role and give me the confidence that I can succeed."

Another way of offering support is by providing a safe environment where concerns can be openly discussed in a confidential way. One interviewee said that a coach can help to release stress: "It serves like a valve." The coach creates a safe environment where the leader's struggles and frustrations can be discussed and reframed into something positive. The coach can help the leader test his assumptions on certain behaviors and actions from stakeholders and create an approach and plan to move forward. Conflicts and frustrations usually arise from differences in how people see the world and how they grew up; the family, geographical location, education and work experience. The coach can help the executive to see different perspectives and worldviews and build understanding and awareness.

Looking at the CCCP coaching competencies, the competencies presence, relating, listening and questioning are essential to create a safe environment for the executive to discuss issues openly.

Question 2: What would and ideal coaching engagement, with the goal to support executives in business transformations, look like? This section explores what the interviewees said about their ideal coaching program, it compares the results with the CCCP competencies and process and it includes comments from my own experience as a change consultant and executive coach.

THEMES

1. Formal or informal coaching?

Interviewees made the case for both. One interviewee said that informal coaching happens all the time during work. Executives take the responsibility to coach project team members.

Another interviewee confirmed the informality of coaching. "It happens all the time." Coaching is done by everybody, regardless of position in the organization. If someone needs help with a topic or skill, someone else who has the knowledge can act as a coach. Informal coaching has the advantage of being more fluid, it can happen ad hoc and as needed. The process of pairing people happens more naturally. People who think they need coaching on a certain topic seek out people in the organization who can act as a coach. This process of matching people spontaneously doesn't feel forced and it can create healthy coaching relationships.

Another interviewee preferred a formal coaching program: "A formal program will incentivize executives to reserve time to prepare for and attend coaching sessions." Several aspects of a coaching engagement can be formalized. Firstly, the coach – coachee relationship itself can be formalized. This was crucial for one of the interviewees. The relationship must be established before the kick of off the transformation/change effort. Besides the relationship itself, the (contract, objectives of the coaching engagement) and the process (topics of discussion, number and duration of meetings, action plan to track progress against the objectives) must be established between the two parties. The interviewee mentioned an official sign off as part of the set-up of the coaching engagement.

The CCCP program offers a formal coaching relationship with coach competencies and three phases and steps. It is clear from the interviews that it is not an either/or with regards to the formality of a coaching relationship. Informal coaching happens all the time and should continue to happen. Coaching is a way for people to learn about themselves and from others and this should be encouraged. A formal coaching process increases the chances that learning takes place for the coachee and benefits the transformation and the organization. There is too much at stake in a business transformation to rely on informal coaching.

My experience suggests several reasons in favor of a formal coaching program:

- With a formal program, benefits and results are tracked and made visible. It creates an extra layer of administrative work, but it is worth it.

- There needs to be a central point of coordination of the program. It is important to check in with the coaches to understand how the participants are progressing.

- Progress updates with stakeholders and managers of the coachees help to move the program forward. Once you allow participants to fall behind, the coaching program may lose its credibility.

- The formality of the program also protects the dollars invested in the coaches, the program design and the administration.

2. Standard or customized Coaching Program

A few interviewees prefer a customized coaching program over a standard program. The customized approach is designed to address the specific needs of the transformation/change effort. Variables mentioned are: cost, complexity of the implementation, geography, scope, receptiveness of the coaches, people who are at the receiving end of the change, the experience of the project leaders, project teams, and change leaders.

One interviewee had an interesting perspective about the timing of the coaching. The interviewee suggested that coaching should take place at the moment of impact. Both the project organization and those who are required to change are impacted at various times during the transformation. Transformations often span multiple years and impact will be experienced by different groups at different times. For the project organization the impact happens at the start of every phase in the project (for large system implementations this can be Kick Off, Design, Test, and Deployment). At these moments the impact of the activities of the success of the project is high and the effects of coaching will be most impactful.

For those who are at the receiving end of the change, a similar argument holds. The business will start to feel the impact during the deployment phase of the project. Although I would argue it starts sooner (during stakeholder analysis and engagement, design sessions and during testing). Even though the real impact doesn't occur during these phases people will start to understand what the changes are going to be and coaching (at least the senior leaders/change leaders) will increase the preparedness of people for the impacts further down the road. It is true that larger groups of people will feel the impacts when the deployment starts. During this phase coaching must be intensified to support/guide people through the changes.

3. Internal or external coaches

Interviewees had different views about the benefits of internal versus external coaches. One interviewee preferred internal coaches. An internal coach understands the culture of the organization. An external coach doesn't have enough time to understand the culture to be successful. Other reasons mentioned to use internal coaches were the existence of an internal coaching program, access to a pool of internal coaches and the fact that internal coaches use techniques/tools used on previous transformations.

Another interviewee opines that an external coach is more effective than an internal coach. External coaches are outsiders of the organization. They are neutral and help the executive maintain objectivity by offering different perspectives. The interviewee stated that the external coach is better able to drive transformational change because he is not part of the system. An internal coach has the disadvantage of being influenced too much by the organizational culture.

One interviewee suggested external coaches are needed to work with senior leaders who are considered major blockers to the success of the transformation. The external coach can apply pressure to the executive in making clear that the blocker will not be successful if he/she doesn't change his/her behavior.

4. Characteristics of change leaders and their coaches

The interviewees described the characteristics of change leaders and their coaches as follows:

Change Leader	Coach
• Self-sufficiency	• Some people just have the innate skills to be a coach
• Understand both the detail and the big picture	• Empathy
• Go the extra mile, do what it takes to be successful	• Ability to listen
• Be passionate about the objectives of the transformation and have complete commitment to the success of the project	• Communicate directly and clearly back to the person being coached
	• Ability to work with the people around the coachee
• Technical knowledge	• Understanding of the strategic objectives of the transformation
• Self-confidence	
• Ability to work with all parties involved to get it done	• Being Practical

Interviewers also responded who would benefit the most from coaching. One interviewee said that "Anybody who needs it should get coaching." Another interviewee wants blockers to a transformation to be coached. Blockers are those executives whose leadership style, experience/knowledge or attitude towards the transformation negatively impacts the success of the transformation. Receptiveness to coaching is also important to consider when considering an executive for coaching. "If someone is not receptive to it, forget about it," said one interviewee.

One interviewee stated that coaching doesn't work for very senior leaders. "They are too senior to be coached. Coaching is more suited for executives who are at the beginning of their (executive) careers."

5. Mentoring versus Coaching

Some interviewees said that the definition of coaching used by the ICF is not useful. They felt that mentoring is better suited for coaching in transformations than ICFs definition of coaching. Change Leaders in transformations have to be taught how to implement change. This means that the coaches/mentors have to be experts in change management. As stated before, a hybrid model is a better solution. Becoming an expert in change management as a change leader isn't a guarantee you will be successful in the transformation. There are other qualities needed, such as strategic thinking, interpersonal skills, communication skills, executive presence and tolerance for ambiguity, to name a few. These competencies can best be taught by a coach, not a mentor. The leadership development program I co-created had both coaches and mentors helping participants with technical skills (mentor) and leadership skills (coach).

Another limitation of the ICF definition in the context of a business transformation is the focus on the potential of the individual, not the organization. This focus is too narrow in the context of executive coaching for business transformations. Expanding the definition to include a focus on groups and organizations will expand the scope of the field of executive coaching and help link the areas of change management and executive coaching.

Summary and Conclusions

This chapter examined how executive coaching contributes to the success of business transformations. As a change consultant and executive coach, working with change leaders in business transformations, I was interested in finding out how executive coaches can contribute to the success of business transformations and how an engagement could look like. Six executives were interviewed at a global consumer goods company. The executives were asked 1. How executive coaching can contribute to their success as change leaders? and , 2. How does an ideal coaching engagement look like? Themes from the interviews, unique perspectives from the interviewees, comparisons of the results with concepts of the CCCP program, and experiences from the author were presented in this chapter.

Firstly, all interviewees agreed that having a coach during their role as change leader would have helped them both personally and with the business transformation. Specifically, Executive Coaching helps to realize the vision of the transformation. Coaching further helps to change behaviors and assist with the executives learning certain skills and competencies. Coaching helps to sustain a culture needed for successful transformations and helps executives to manage relationships.

Lastly, coaching offers a safe environment for executives to release team and analyze situations and experiences from different angles to gain a better understanding and make more informed decisions. Kotter's model confirms that having a clear vision is essential to any business transformation and it is great to see that the interviewed executives see a coach playing an important role in realizing the vision. The CCCP competencies of reframing, business acumen and testing assumptions are very suitable to help the executives create and communicate the vision.

The interviewees had different opinions about how to design coaching programs. Some preferred informal coaching, others felt coaching should be formal. Some thought that internal coaches are preferred because of knowing and understanding organizational culture, others believe external coaches can apply pressure to executives in case they are considered "blockers" or can provide an external, more objective perspective on any situation.

In my experience, a formal program is preferred when the stakes are high. Informal coaching happens all the time and should be encouraged and stimulated. Formal coaching will pay attention to the objectives of a transformation and making executives successful in their roles in achieving the vision of the transformation. As a next step to further the understanding of how executive coaching can assist change leaders, research must be conducted in which coaches are paired with change leaders to determine the effects of coaching on the personal success of the executive and the success of the transformation.

REFERENCES

Covey, Stephen M.R. (2006). The Speed of Trust, the one thing that changes everything. *New York, Simon & Schuster, Inc.*

Kotter, J. P. (1995). Leading change: Why transformation efforts fail. *Harvard business review*, 73(2), 59-67.

Kotter, J. P. (2007). Leading change. *HBR's 10 must Reads on Change*, 2.

Materials from the Columbia Coaching Certification Program's Front-End Coach Intensives Spring 2010

Stefan Hendriks worked for Ernst & Young, Cap Gemini and Deloitte as a human capital consultant for more than ten years in Europe and in the USA. He worked for clients in banking, consumer goods and pharmaceuticals in Ireland, Sweden, Belgium, The Netherlands, France, the UK and the USA. He has experience in change management, Leadership Development, 360 Feedback & Hogan Assessments, Diversity and Inclusion, Organization Design and Executive Coaching. He completed the Columbia Coaching Certification Program in 2011. He currently is an independent consultant and is pursuing a doctorate in Adult Learning and Leadership at Teachers College, Columbia University.

ABOUT ANNE POWER

Anne Power has more than twenty-five years of experience coaching leaders and teams, consulting in organizations, and teaching, both across the U.S. and around the globe. Highlights of her experience include serving as the first woman Visiting Fellow at the Department of Justice, as president of Cincinnati Public Schools Board of Education, and as a board member of The American Center for International Leadership. She helped design and develop the Columbia Coaching Certification Program and has taught in the program since its inception. She also developed the Urban Leader as Coach program in the Urban Educator Leadership Doctoral Program at Teachers College, Columbia University, as well as the curriculum for a health and wellness coaching certification program for the Center for Integral Health at National University.

Anne holds a doctorate from the Department of Organization and Leadership, Teachers College, Columbia University. She is the co-author (with Terrence Maltbia) of *A Leader's Guide to Leveraging Diversity* (2009).

Made in the USA
Columbia, SC
16 June 2021